EGYPTIAN
PAGANISM

for Beginners

About the Authors

Jocelyn Almond is an Archpriestess-Hierophant in the Fellowship of Isis, and teaches Magi Degree courses in meditation and magic through her Fellowship Lyceum.

Keith Seddon is the director of the Stoic Foundation and Professor of Philosophy at Warnborough University.

Jointly, Jocelyn Almond and Keith Seddon have written books about the Tarot and Egyptian Paganism. Each holds a PhD in philosophy. As a happily married pagan couple, they share teaching experience in a range of subjects, including academic philosophy, topics in humanities, and New Age studies.

EGYPTIAN
PAGANISM

for Beginners

Bring the Gods & Goddesses into Daily Life

JOCELYN ALMOND & KEITH SEDDON

2004
Llewellyn Publications
St. Paul, Minnesota 55164-0383, U.S.A.

First Edition
First Printing, 2004

Book design by Donna Burch
Cover collage created using images © SuperStock, Digital Stock, & Corel
Cover design by Kevin R. Brown
Interior illustrations by Kevin R. Brown
Editing by Jennifer Gehlhar

Library of Congress Cataloging-in-Publication Data

Almond, Jocelyn.
    Egyptian paganism for beginners : bring the gods & goddesses into daily life
/ Jocelyn Almond & Keith Seddon.—1st ed.
        p.   cm.
    Includes bibliographical references.
    ISBN 0-7387-0438-5
        1. Magic, Egyptian. 2. Gods, Egyptian. 3. Goddesses, Egyptian. 4. Pagan-
ism. I. Seddon, Keith, 1956–. II. Title.

BF1591.A46 2004
299'.31—dc22   2004048329

Llewellyn Publications
A Division of Llewellyn Worldwide, Ltd.
P.O. Box 64383, Dept. 0-7387-0438-5
St. Paul, MN 55164-0383, U.S.A.
www.llewellyn.com

Printed in the United States of America

Other Books by Jocelyn Almond
and Keith Seddon

The Book of Egyptian Ritual:
Simple Rites and Blessings for Everyday
[previously published as *An Egyptian Book of Shadows*]
(Thorsons, 2002)

Understanding Tarot
(Aquarian Press, 1991)

Tarot for Lovers
[previously published as *Tarot for Relationships*]
(Thorsons, 1995)

Contents

Contents

Contents

Acknowledgments

The authors are very grateful to the following publishers for their kind cooperation in granting permission for the use of extracts from their publications to compose the rites in this book.

Aris & Phillips (Oxbow Books) for extracts from R. O. Faulkner, *The Ancient Egyptian Coffin Texts*, 3 vols. (1973, 1977, 1978.) © R. O. Faulkner, 1973, 1977, 1978.

E. J. Brill for an extract translated by J. F. Borghouts, *Ancient Egyptian Magical Texts*, 1978. © E. J. Brill, 1978.

Cornell University Press for a text about Neith translated by L. H. Lesko, *Religion in Ancient Egypt: Gods, Myths, and Personal Practice*, Byron Shafer, ed., repr., 1991. © Cornell University, 1991. Used by permission of the publisher, Cornell University Press.

Editions Robert Laffont (Simon & Schuster) for extracts from Christian Jacq, *The Living Wisdom of Ancient Egypt*, 1999. © Editions Robert Laffont, 1998.

Professor John L. Foster (Scholars Press) for extracts translated by John L. Foster, *Hymns, Prayers, and Songs: An Anthology of Ancient Egyptian Lyric Poetry*, Susan Tower Hollis, ed., 1995. © John L. Foster, 1995.

Oxford University Press for extracts from R. O. Faulkner, *The Ancient Egyptian Pyramid Texts*, 1969. © Oxford University Press, 1969.

Routledge (Thomson Publishing) for a text about Neith from B. J. Kemp, *Ancient Egypt: Anatomy of a Civilization*, 1989. © B. J. Kemp, 1989.

Tempus Publishing for an extract from Barbara Watterson, *The Temple of Horus at Edfu*, 1998. © Barbara Watterson, 1998.

Thames and Hudson for an extract from R. T. Rundle Clark, *Myth and Symbolism in Ancient Egypt*, 1959. © Thames and Hudson Ltd., 1959.

University of California Press for extracts from Miriam Lichtheim, *Ancient Egyptian Literature*, 3 vols. (University of California Press, 1975, 1976, 1980.) © Regents of the University of California, 1973–1980.

University of Chicago Press for extracts edited by Hans Dieter Betz, *The Greek Magical Papyri in Translation*, 1996. © The University of Chicago, 1992.

Extracts From the Following Works Have Also Been Included

Arcana, E. A. Wallis Budge, ed., *Book of the Dead*, 1989.

Citadel Press, E. A. Wallis Budge, *Egyptian Religion*, 1996.

Dover Publications, E. A. Wallis Budge, *The Gods of the Egyptians*, 2 vols., 1969.

Dover Publications, E. A. Wallis Budge, *An Introduction to Ancient Egyptian Literature*, 1997.

Acknowledgments

The authors have made all reasonable efforts to contact and request permissions from the copyright holders of extracts used in this book. If through error or omission any copyright holders have not been contacted, the publishers would be very pleased to hear from them so that appropriate acknowledgments may be included in future editions.

PART ONE

CHAPTER ONE

CONCEPTS OF GOD

The ancient Egyptian religion had many deities, for which the Egyptian word is *neteru* (pronounced "neecheroo"). Some neteru are the same deity or *neter* (pronounced "neecher"), under different names and forms, and some are assimilated with other deities. Surviving myths concern the activities of only a select few of the major neteru, while there are scores of minor ones known only from their names appearing in passing, frequently in an obscure context, in sacred texts. For this reason, Egyptian writings, such as the *Book of the Dead*, may seem baffling to the non-scholarly reader, who finds them swarming with hoards of divine and demonic beings with weird names and titles, behaving in surprising or incomprehensible ways. (We refer often in this book to translations by E. A. Wallis Budge of the *Book of the Dead*, 1895 and 1989.) Sometimes the same function is shared by more than one deity. For instance, Ra, Khepera, Sekhmet, Hathor, Horus, and Atum all preside over the sun; Thoth and Khonsu are both lunar deities; Geb, Aker, and Tatenen are all divinities of the earth; and Isis and Osiris are deities of almost everything.

The frequent crossover of roles and duplication of function currently found among neteru may have been inevitable. The reasons for this curious theological evolution have sometimes been attributed to merging cults, regional variations, and syncretism in a religion of enormous longevity. Egyptian civilization endured for over three thousand years, from the thirty-first century BC to the first century AD. Different deities and cult centers came to prominence at different times, giving rise to various adjustments and assimilations. Some deities were worshipped all over Egypt and had a shrine in every major temple, while others were of local importance only. Not all neteru had god-like status—some, such as the Sons of Horus, seem more like angels than gods, and some never had cult centers or temples of their own, but were worshipped only within the cults of major neteru. Rather than seeing Egyptian Paganism as a collection of competing cults, it may be more enlightening to regard it as a religion with a number of complementary theological strands finding expression through four major religious centers of learning: Heliopolis, where the Ennead was venerated; Memphis, the cult center of Ptah; Thebes, where Amun was worshipped; and Hermopolis, the cult center of the Ogdoad and the god Thoth.

According to orthodox Egyptology, different deities came to prominence at different times because of changes in politics, cultural fashion, and the preferences of whichever pharaoh happened to be on the throne. There is yet another alternative view. Some writers have suggested that the shift of emphasis from the cult of one deity to that of another occurred in accordance with the zodiacal cycle of the ages, so that pairs of deities were worshipped in the Age of Gemini, the twins; Osiris was worshipped as a bull in the Age of Taurus, the bull; and Amun was worshipped as a ram in the Age of Aries, the ram (Cooke, 1979 [1931], p. 20; Clark, 2000, pp. 136–7). The zodiacal age is determined by the sign of the zodiac (constellation) that is on the eastern horizon when and where the sun rises at the spring equinox (in March), and this changes according to a phenomenon called precession, which makes the sun appear to move backward through the zodiacal cycle as the millennia pass.

A religion that involves the veneration of many deities is polytheistic. Polytheism is a striking feature of the ancient Pagan religions, distinguishing them from the more modern monotheistic religions of Judaism, Christianity, and Islam, in which one deity is worshipped. On the face of it, ancient Egyptian religion appears to be a form of polytheism, but it does not conform to a standard model of such a religion in the way that, for instance, the ancient Greek religion does.

That is, it does not have a clear pantheon of individual deities, each with his or her particular role, headed by a chief god. The peculiar features of Egyptian religion have led some Egyptologists to believe that it was actually a form of monotheism. Erik Hornung, in his influential book *Conceptions of God in Ancient Egypt*, has argued that if this is taken to mean that the Egyptians worshiped a major god in addition to the numerous gods they are known to have worshiped, then it is untrue that they were monotheists. He specifically states that they did not place one of the gods as a chief god above all the rest. A very distinctive feature of ancient Egyptian religion is that any one of the main deities could, on any particular occasion, be the Supreme Being. A deity was the Supreme Being in his or her own temple, and each deity was addressed in prayer by a priest or individual devotee as if that deity were the one and only Supreme Being. The same practice is found in Hinduism today. The terms used by Hornung that apply to this form of religion are "monolatry" and "henotheism."

As a monolatrous religion, ancient Egyptian religion involves the worship of many individual deities, while at the same time it can be seen as a religion of one Deity—a mighty, ineffable power that manifests everywhere and in everything, having multitudes of forms and multitudes of names—who is Khepera, "who came into being as the things which came into being, and . . . came into being in the forms of the one who comes into being"; and who is Neith, "who is all that has been, and is, and shall be"; and

Sekhmet-Bast-Ra, "superior to whom the gods cannot be"; and Isis, "Lady of All in the Secret Place"; and Osiris, "King of Eternity, Lord of Everlasting . . . King of Kings, Lord of Lords, Ruler of Rulers"; and Amun, "the Hidden One"; and Neb-er-tcher, "the Lord of All." Each of the major neteru can represent the Supreme Being, each showing a slightly different facet of the One who is unknowable and inconceivable in his or her entirety. The neteru retain their individual identities, so the devotee is able to encounter the One in a very personal and intimate way.

In the form of Egyptian religion practiced at Heliopolis, a group of deities called the Ennead was worshipped. This idea was copied at other cult centers. In *Egyptian Light and Hebrew Fire*, Karl W. Luckert has shown that this concept can be interpreted as a single deity expressing itself in both genders through several generations of gods and goddesses. We shall explain this idea in part two of this book, in the chapters dealing with deities of the Heliopolitan Ennead.

The religion of ancient Egypt is a Pagan religion, which means that its deities manifest within the natural world as the gods and goddesses of the sun, moon, stars, planets, and all life on Earth. Immanence, the manifestation of Deity in nature, is a characteristic of Pagan religions in general, distinguishing them from the monotheistic religions that treat Deity as transcendent or outside the material world. However, in Pagan religions, Deity is not entirely immanent (this would be pantheism), but has a transcendent aspect, in that the Supreme Being is addressed and related to as a person, and not regarded as just an impersonal force or energy.

Part two of this book contains material for the veneration of some of the major Egyptian neteru, concentrating on those neteru most popular with Pagans today. As this is not intended to be a dictionary of gods and goddesses, the neteru are not presented in alphabetical order, but in the order that we believe is going to be most helpful for clearly explaining the nature of ancient Egyptian religious beliefs and practices, showing an overall view of the religion, even though only a small selection of the neteru is featured. In the remaining chapters of part one, we provide guidelines for practicing a modern form of Paganism based on ancient Egyptian religion. We find this approach suitable for Pagans today, who are very often following a private spiritual path as individuals, without the benefit of a temple or the support of a group.

CHAPTER TWO

KA, SEKHEM, AND THE HEAVENLY KINE

Psychics, mystics, magicians, and those who meditate often speak of energy centers in the human body. A psychic-etheric form of energy flows through these centers and may be used in altered states of consciousness to produce various psychic and magical effects. These energy centers are generally referred to as *chakras*—a Sanskrit word meaning "wheel"—because people with psychic vision see chakras spinning like wheels.

There is evidence that the ancient Egyptians may have had similar ideas about a psychic-etheric form of energy within the body and its location at certain points on the body. To understand this, we need to examine three of their concepts: *ka*, *sekhem*, and the Heavenly Kine.

The word *ka* is often translated as "double," conveying the impression that the ancient Egyptians believed that each person had some sort of replica self on a spiritual plane. The ka (double) comes into existence when an individual is born, and has a protective function, rather like a guardian angel, watching over and guiding the individual to whom it is attached. The concepts of an etheric body or etheric double, a spirit guide, the higher self, and the Chinese *chi* (vital force), all have similarities to the Egyptian ka. This is quite a confusing idea, which upon first thought does not seem to make much sense in a modern context.

In fact, the concept of the ka is rather more complex. Ka is sometimes spoken of as a general spiritual force or energy. Because of the similarity of the word *ka* to the Egyptian word for "bull," and because the bull was used as a symbol of male potency (being big, strong, and virile), it has been suggested that the ka was also associated with male potency (Lurker, 1982, p. 73). It seems that the Egyptians may have been using one word for several different, yet related, concepts, as we use the word "spirit."

The hieroglyphic symbol for ka, a pair of extended arms, represents an embrace. People were depicted sitting in the lap of the ka like a child embraced by its mother. To put one's arms round someone in the ka embrace was symbolic of imparting vital energy to that person. In the *Pyra-*

mid Texts, Utterance 600, (trans. Faulkner, 1985) it is said that the Creator, Atum, put his arms around his two children, Shu and Tefnut, when he first made them, "in the form of a ka symbol, in order to transmit his divine essence to them."

In one respect, ka is the etheric body and an aspect of the self of each individual. Ka is the life force that comes from the Creator, and it is able to pass from one person to another through bodily contact. On the other hand, to go to one's ka was an expression meaning to die, indicating that the ka was also a sustaining spiritual source associated with the otherworld and the ancestors. The word *ka* is also a component of the word *heka* (magic), spelled with two hieroglyphs—a piece of twisted flax, and the ka symbol of the arms.

The ancient Egyptians had a concept related to ka, called *sekhem*, which denotes a vital force within the body. This word is usually translated as "power," and is the root of the name of the goddess Sekhmet. It may be thought that the term *sekhem* approximates in meaning to the word (often used in yoga), *kundalini*, which refers to the body's psychic-etheric energy (Clark, 2000, p. 303). Although we cannot be sure that the ancient Egyptian words *ka* and *sekhem* mean the exact equivalent of terms we use today for such concepts, one gains the general impression that the ancient Egyptians were aware of the same vital, creative force that is recognized by modern healers and magicians—the force experienced in the body, which flows in the spine and passes out through the hands in acts of magic and healing. It is this energy that is visualized when casting a circle, consecrating ritual equipment, and empowering magical objects, such as talismans. The ancient Egyptians called energy *heka* in the context of using it for what we would call magical purposes; *ka* when referring to the individual spirit of a living being; and *sekhem* when referring to etheric energy as a life force.

In the Hindu practice of kundalini-yoga there are seven main chakras or psychic-etheric energy centers in the body. These are imagined or seen clairvoyantly as colored points along the body and up into the head. They are often colored according to the sequence of a rainbow, although some people prefer to use a different sequence of colors in accordance with an older tradition. Generally speaking, the lower chakras should be warm colors (reds and yellows) and the upper chakras should be cool colors (blues and violets), while the heart chakra should be green. The chakras are situated at the "crown" (on top of the head, visualized as white or violet); "third eye" (between the brows, indigo or violet); "throat" (in the middle of the neck, blue); "heart" (in the middle of the chest, green); "solar plexus" (at the midriff, yellow); "sacral center" (below the navel, orange); and "base" (at the perineum, red).

The ancient Egyptian idea of the "Knots of the Heavenly Kine" has been linked to the idea of the chakra system (Jacq, 1985, pp. 57–8). *Coffin Texts*, Spell 407, (trans. Faulkner, 1973) is concerned with these, but unless one is prepared to experiment, there is a problem using this spell to awaken the chakras. If the seven paragraphs in this text naming the Knots do refer to the chakras, it is not clear which Knots relate to which chakras. The names of the Knots appear to be: Set, great Longhorn dwelling in the northern sky; Loud-voiced, greatly majestic, sitting in the midst of darkness; Lord of Splendor; Heights of Neith; Earth-god; Neith, Mistress of *Netchset*; and Lord of the Seed of the Five Bulls.

Another similarity between the Egyptian and Hindu religions is found in the significance of serpents. The kundalini is an energy likened to a serpent coiled in the base chakra, which rises during mystical awakening or may be gently stimulated through meditational practices. Exercises that involve visualization of light, water, or fire flowing through the spine are used by modern meditators to encourage the free flow of etheric energy that is believed to occur in the spine naturally. An indication that the Egyptians had a similar concept of this serpent power is their use of the *uraeus* (cobra symbol)—the sacred serpent on the brow of the king and various neteru. In the case of Ra-Atum, the chief neter of Heliopolis (Iunu, On), the "serpent of terror" on his brow is an Eye goddess; originally one of his own eyes that he sent in search of his two children when they were swept off the primeval mound into the waters of Nun. When the Eye came back with the lost children, she was furious to find that Ra-Atum had grown a replacement Eye; so, to placate her, he placed the original Eye on his brow in the form of a serpent. This could be an image of the serpent power rising up from the base of the spine to the third eye chakra. Other notable neteru who are depicted with this uraeus are Osiris, who is often identified with the Creator; Isis, who is the Lady of Heka; and Sekhmet, the fiery lioness who is identified with the Eye itself and represents the power of the sun.

Because of the similarities between Egyptian symbolism and the symbolism of the Eastern chakra system, it is acceptable to use the chakras in meditation and magic when working on the Egyptian spiritual path. The chakras are often visualized, or seen with psychic vision, as small flowers (traditionaly lotuses), and may have their petals open or closed. When people speak of "opening up" to do psychic work and "closing down" afterward, they are referring to the opening and closing of the chakras, although those at the crown and base are always left open.

At the start of a ritual or meditation, it is a good idea to sit quietly for a few minutes and visualize the chakras opening and shining as a transparent clear light in the corresponding color. Energy should be visualized as flowing from the earth, up the legs into the spine, and white light should be visualized as shining down from above, onto the crown chakra. At the end of a session, all the chakras, except the base and crown, should be visualized as closing gently. Eating or drinking something soon after will bring the meditator safely back to the material realm.

CHAPTER THREE

CASTING A MAGIC CIRCLE

A magic circle is used by modern Pagans to create a sacred space in a mundane environment and provide psychic protection if any magic work is in progress. The ancient Egyptian priesthood did not cast magic circles because they were working in consecrated temples. However, it has been suggested that Egyptian magicians, especially when working outside a temple, may have cast circles (Pinch, 1994, p. 78). Unless you have a special dedicated temple in your home, it is best to cast a circle. Works of Low Magic (practical magic) should always be done in a circle.

You will need four candles or tea candles for the four quarters, and two candles for the altar or shrine, an image of the deity, and preferably a wand and *sistrum* (an Egyptian sacred rattle, shaken to banish evil influences and attract the attention of the deities). If you do not have a wand at present, use your index finger. Egyptian magicians used a flat, curved wand, resembling a boomerang, or else a wand in the form of a snake. The magician's wand is used for the channeling and direction of energy to a desired location. A sistrum may be improvised from anything that rattles— even some small beads inside a tin. The candles on the altar or shrine, placed one on either side of the deity image, may be a color associated with the neter you wish to invoke, which can be determined by seeing how the neter is portrayed in Egyptian art; otherwise, for any particular rite, you may use white. The tea candles may be placed in colored holders to represent each of the four elements or colored candles may be substituted: yellow for air in the east, red for fire in the south, blue for water in the west, and black for earth in the north. (However, when performing a rite of Low Magic, as described in part one, chapter 7, the colors should be blue for air, red for fire, green for water, and yellow for earth.) The shrine or altar should preferably be placed in the east, the direction of sunrise, or else so that you are facing toward Egypt; but if this is not possible, all directions have some sacred significance.

Calling the Elemental Powers

Light the candles or tea candles at the four quarters, but leave the candles on the altar unlit when you start. Face the altar and compose yourself, relax. Visualize a white light of purity shining down from above. It comes from a divine source and bathes you and the room in its cleansing power, removing all unwanted influences from the vicinity. Imagine the divine light entering through the top of your head and flowing down your spine, awakening the latent psychic-etheric energy that is in your spine. A force also rises up your body from the earth. Imagine these forces within your body, imbuing you with power.

Take up your wand or use your finger, and turning clockwise, face east. Point your wand or finger toward the east and visualize the power flowing out toward where you point. Moving clockwise, draw the circle around your working area, from east to south, to west, to north, to east. As you draw it, visualize it as a line of bright bluish-white light flowing from the tip of your wand or finger, emanating from the power circling in your spine. Take your time to do this, pausing at each quarter if necessary—you may need to allow power to gather before you continue. When you have completed the circle, see it as a line round the circumference of a great protective sphere that encompasses you and your place of working, creating a sacred space within it.

Calling the Sons of Horus

Always turning clockwise, take the sistrum, face east, and shake it. Say: "Hail to you, Lords and Ladies of the East, Powers of Air! Hail, Lord Qebhsennuf! Please be present at this sacred place and witness this rite." You need to "vibrate" (chant or sing so that you sense a vibration in your throat and chest) the sacred name "Kebs-noof," and project the sound out onto the astral plane or realm of the imagination. The sound does not have to be loud in actuality, but it should be imagined as loud enough to call the powers of elemental air to you. As you chant this name three or four times, visualize Lord Qebhsennuf approaching in the form of a falcon—a golden bird of prey. He comes to rest at the edge of the circle as a tall, falcon-headed man, and behind him you can see a sunny sky with windswept clouds. (Close your eyes if it helps to visualize this.) You may "hear" clairaudiently a greeting from the neter. Reply politely, thanking him for coming (you may reply with your "inner voice" rather than speaking aloud).

Turn south, shake the sistrum. Say: "Hail to you, Lords and Ladies of the South, Powers of Fire! Hail, Lord Duamutef! Please be present at this sacred place and witness this rite." Vibrate the name "Doo-a-moo-tef." Visualize him as a black jackal—a slim, doglike animal resembling a greyhound with erect, pointed ears and a bushy tail—approaching through a desert landscape. He comes to rest at the edge of the circle as a jackal-headed man (or woman, as this neter is

18

sometimes female), seen against a background of flames. If he greets you, thank him for coming.

Carry out a similar procedure in the west, calling on the powers of water and Lord Imsety. Vibrate his name "Im-set-ee." See him as a bearded man standing on the seashore with the waves behind him.

Repeat the procedure in the north, but this time calling on the powers of earth and Lord Hapi. His name should be vibrated "Hah-pee." Visualize the neter approaching in the form of a baboon or ape. He stands on the edge of the circle as a baboon-headed man, seen against a background of plants and trees.

These four guardian neteru, Qebhsennuf, Duamutef, Imsety, and Hapi, are called the Four Sons of Horus. (Incidentally, there is some disagreement about which Son of Horus symbolizes which element or cardinal point. Some people prefer to attribute the elements to different cardinal points when performing an Egyptian rite. We have found this particular arrangement to be effective, but you may prefer a different one.)

Turn clockwise and face the shrine or altar. Shake the sistrum. Say:

> The heavens are opened,
> The earth is opened,
> The West is opened,
> The East is opened,
> The southern half of heaven is opened,

The northern half of heaven is opened,
The doors are opened,
And the gates are thrown wide open to Ra
As he cometh forth from the horizon.

—Book of the Dead, *chapter 130, translation by E. A. Wallis Budge.*

(The doors mentioned are the doors of the shrine, so leave this line out if your shrine has no doors or they are not open. If you are performing the rite at night, you may prefer to substitute the name of the moon god, Thoth or Khonsu, for that of Ra.)

Shake the sistrum. The circle is now cast. Light the candles on the shrine or altar. Say:

The shining Eye of Horus cometh.
The brilliant Eye of Horus cometh.
It cometh in peace;
It sendeth forth rays of light unto Ra in the horizon,
And it destroyeth the powers of Set according to the
    decree.
It leadeth them on and it taketh possession of him,
And its flame is kindled against him.
Its flame cometh and goeth about and bringeth
    adoration;
It cometh and goeth about heaven in the train of Ra
Upon the two hands of thy two sisters, O Ra.
The Eye of Horus liveth,
Yea, liveth within the great hall;

The Eye of Horus liveth,

Yea, liveth!

—Book of the Dead, *chapter 137B, translation by E. A. Wallis Budge.*

(This spell banishes the harmful influences of the god Set, so is not suitable for use if you are conducting a rite to invoke Set himself.)

The first time you cast the circle, you may like to sit in it quietly for a while to see how it feels, and try to clear your mind without doing any of the other exercises. Otherwise you may do the chakra exercises while in the circle. If you invoke any deity, you should always thank him or her at the end of the rite.

Closing the Circle

Go round the circle counter-clockwise, starting in the east and pausing at each quarter to thank the respective elemental powers and neter. For example, in the east, shake the sistrum and say: "Lords and Ladies of the East, Powers of Air, and Lord Qebhsennuf, thank you for attending this rite. Hail and farewell!" Visualize the neter departing, taking the elementals with him as the door to the elemental world closes. Extinguish the candle or tea candle as this happens. Use the energy to send a word of blessing to the elementals. Finally say, "May I go forth with the Divine blessing!" Otherwise, send a healing thought to those in need —candles in a rite should not be blown out unless they are used in this way. If you do not send a blessing, snuff out the candles on the altar.

CHAPTER FOUR

MAKING A SHRINE

The act of making a shrine can be remarkably effective in helping one to establish a devotional path, yet this practical aspect of religion is often neglected. The very word "shrine" seems to have become debased in our culture, taking on a morbid air, as it tends to be associated with dead people—in particular, saints and Christian martyrs. Christian shrines often contain relics, such as bones or even the remains of the whole body of the saint to whom the shrine is dedicated.

The sort of shrine we are concerned with here, however, is not of this nature. It may be regarded as a small, permanent altar to the neter of one's choice, to be a place of life and energy, where the devotee may encounter the neter as a living presence. Having a shrine in one's home is a constant reminder of the particular path that one has chosen, and so is of great help to the beginner on a spiritual path, who may experience temptations to lapse if a regular pattern of devotion has not yet been established. The shrine also becomes a physical marker of one's spiritual growth and changing relationship to Deity as its contents increase and change over the years.

The shrine does not have to be an elaborate affair. It should be large enough to contain at least a central motif as the focus of attention—such as a statuette or picture of the deity chosen or a sacred symbol, such as an ankh—plus objects symbolizing the four elements of earth, air, fire, and water. It should not be so large as to be intrusive or inconvenient in a normal room used for other purposes. At the same time, it is important to keep the shrine exclusively as a shrine and not to allow irrelevant objects, such as coffee cups or ashtrays, to find their way onto it, which may happen if it is on a table in a living room. It may also be necessary to consider having some sort of cover for the shrine, so that it can be concealed from the gaze of family members and visitors who may not understand one's religion. A cover can also have a psychological effect on the devotee, so that taking off the cover, by association after months of practice, will stimulate the opening of the psychic centers in one's body, and putting back the cover will help one to "close down" psychically afterward.

For these reasons, we once had a shrine inside a drop-front bureau, which could be easily opened for devotional practice and closed at a moment's notice to shield the shrine from unexpected casual visitors. Now, however, we have adapted an old music cabinet for the purpose by painting it turquoise blue on the inside and decorating the outside with Egyptian designs. A cupboard or a recess with a curtain over it are alternative versions of this idea. Care should always be taken to close the shrine only after all candles inside have been extinguished.

It was mentioned above that the shrine should contain an image of the deity chosen. Pictures and statuettes of Egyptian neteru are fairly easy to obtain. Gift, New Age, museum, and a few specialty shops often sell them, although some deities are more elusive than others.

The reason that the image is so important and needs to be three-dimensional if possible is because, when invoking the neter and meditating before the shrine, one needs to be able to visualize that neter. As one's psychic powers develop through regular devotion and meditation before a shrine, images may begin to appear in the mind's eye when the physical eyes are closed, and psychic messages may be received, which can be extremely confusing or even dangerous unless one starts from a position of knowing exactly which forces one is contacting. This is why it is important to invoke Deity. Ask for protection and visualize a clear and unambiguous image of the chosen deity at the beginning of any magical practice involving contact with deities or spirits. A clear image in the shrine can be an invaluable aid to this. In the absence of a physical image of a deity in the shrine, a sacred symbol such as an ankh, Eye of Horus, tet knot

(Buckle of Isis), or scarab will help to provide protection from mischievous entities.

As also mentioned above, a shrine, like an altar, should contain objects representing the four elements—or five elements, if one includes the "element" of spirit. Candles represent fire, incense or perfume represents air, and a small container, such as an egg cup filled with water, may stand for elemental water. For an earth symbol, the ankh is often favored by followers of Egyptian Paganism. The fifth "element" of spirit may be represented by a small amount of oil (almond oil or a special anointing oil) in an egg cup. The small size of the containers makes it possible to have a shrine little more than a foot across—small enough for even the most cramped home.

Incense sticks are the most convenient form of incense to use, but some people feel they are inappropriate for a formal rite. If you decide to use loose incense, be aware that the burner can get extremely hot. Placing a layer of sand in the bottom can improve matters, but it is best to stand the burner on a tile. Self-igniting charcoal discs are the easiest sort to use. Hold the disc with some sugar tongs and put it into a flame until it is well lit. (The fact that it sparks and fizzes at first is not an indication that it is really burning.) Make sure that it is glowing red before placing it in the burner and sprinkling incense on it. Ordinary charcoal needs a little lighter fuel to get it going, but this can be dangerous if not done with care. Also be very careful how you dispose of the charcoal afterward, as it may still be burning when it appears to have turned to ash. Anything you burn or heat should never be put in a waste bin inside the house, unless the object has been left to cool down for a considerable time and doused with water for extra safety.

For those who cannot tolerate incense smoke or who find that it sets off the smoke alarms, perfumed oil used on an aromatherapy evaporator is an acceptable alternative. To use an evaporator, pour some water into the dish on the top, place a few drops of perfumed oil on the water, and light a tea candle underneath. Neither the incense burner nor evaporator should be moved around while hot. The dangers of an incense burner are obvious, but even the water on an evaporator can reach the boiling point, and you can burn yourself if you touch the dish.

With regard to the kind of incense or perfume that should be used, Egyptian blends are most suitable. Kyphi or something formulated for the particular Egyptian deity you are invoking is ideal, but otherwise frankincense is always suitable. Blends of incense and oil for individual deities are available from some specialist occult outlets.

Apart from these basic things, the characteristics of the deity to whom the shrine is dedicated, and the personal taste of the devotee, will determine what else is to go into it. An atmosphere that is conducive to the deity being invoked should be created; for instance, emphasis should be upon any symbolism or totem animals associated with that deity. Color is also an important factor to take into account, as the various neteru are associated with particular colors.

Other items pertinent to one's magical practices may also be kept in the shrine or close to it. All such items should be within the shrine energy field, for a frequently used shrine will become psychically charged and will radiate that energy for a short distance around it. Such items may include Tarot cards and other devices used in divination. Since the shrine will not be large enough to contain all of one's magical equipment, it is best to place in it objects that one is working with at any given time.

When the shrine is first assembled, the area should be purified, especially if it has been previously used for another purpose. This can be done by physically cleaning it (which is also an act symbolic of psychic cleansing) and by burning incense there, before leaving it to "rest" for at least a day. After this, the objects representing the elements, any other objects associated with the chosen deity, and finally the central image or symbol can be placed in it.

A short rite to consecrate the shrine should then be performed. This could be done very simply in one's own words when first setting up the shrine, but to do it properly in authentic Egyptian style, it is necessary to perform a ritual on the statuette(s), which the ancient Egyptians called the Opening of the Mouth.

Having created a shrine, the important thing to do is to keep it alive by cleaning it when necessary, replenishing the water and oil, lighting the candles each day, and burning the incense regularly. Each time the elements are replaced, they should be offered as they were on the first occasion. A short prayer should be said at the shrine each day, if longer devotions are not possible. Meditation sessions should also take place before the shrine. What matters in maintaining a shrine is not spending hours once a month or once a week in elaborate rituals, but just acknowledging Deity at the shrine for a few minutes each day. Regular practice will build up a familiarity, which can have surprisingly beneficial results in terms of one's magical and spiritual development.

Opening of the Mouth

The ritual of the Opening of the Mouth is usually mentioned in connection with ceremonies concerning the mummy of a recently deceased person. However, the Egyptians also used this rite to bring to life statues of the dead and of the neteru. Its origins are very ancient, dating from pre-Dynastic times, but over the centuries this practice developed into a complex rite that included making elaborate offerings. A number of special instruments were used to symbolize the act of splitting open the mouth, the most important among these being a bifurcated flint knife called a *pesesh-kef* and an iron instrument called a *seb-ur*, referred to as an "adze," which may have represented the constellation of Ursa Major.

A central tenet of Egyptian magic is that an image may be magically identified with what it represents, especially if a magical rite is performed on it, using words of power. Even if such a rite was not performed, it was thought that an image might become animated in any case, so for this reason hieroglyphs of lions or snakes were sometimes rendered harmless by drawing them split in two or with a knife through them. If a statue had the Opening of the Mouth ritual performed on it, then it would actually become the person or deity that it represented, its senses awakened so that it could see, hear, and speak. In the Judaeo-Christian tradition, to treat a statue as if it really is God is idolatry, but to the ancient Egyptians and other Pagans, there was no such concept as idolatry. If a statue was "opened" to the spirit of a deity, then the deity actually inhabited the statue, and to all intents and purposes had become that deity.

To perform this rite on your devotional statues, a very simplified version may be used. The statue should be new and cleaned, if it will not be damaged by cleaning. Objects that carry the psychic vibrations of a former user should never be used in ritual magic. To be on the safe side, beginners should avoid using secondhand ritual equipment entirely, including statues.

For this rite, along with the statue and the usual candles, you will need incense (or perfumed oil) and water for the offerings, and preferably wine or beer, and bread, unless the neter is an underworld divinity, when water and dried fruit may be offered. Instead of the knife and adze that the Egyptians would have used, a wand may be substituted.

Place the statue on the shrine or altar. Cast the circle and call on the Sons of Horus in the usual way (see part one, chapter 3). Next you should invoke the deity represented by the statue, and for this rite the aid of Horus will be needed, so he should be invoked too. Say: "Mighty Horus, I invoke you. Please help me to perform this rite." Invoke the other neter in a similar way or use a more elaborate invocation if you wish. (You may find something suitable in part two of this book.)

The full wording for the Opening of the Mouth ritual is in the *Pyramid Texts*, Utterances 20–22. Below is a very simplified version based on it:

> O [statue of *N*], I am Horus. I split open your mouth for you, I split open your eyes for you. O [statue of *N*], I open your mouth with the adze of Wepwawet, with the iron adze with which the mouths of the gods were split open. O Horus, open the mouth of this [statue of *N*]. Horus opens the mouth of this [statue of *N*] with the iron adze he used to open the mouth of Osiris, made from iron which came out of Set—the adze which split open the gods' mouths.

In place of *N*, insert the name of the deity represented by the statue. Point the wand at the mouth and eyes of the statue when speaking the relevant words. You speak as Horus himself, identifying with him. A woman may take this role just as well as a man because it is the function that is being performed and the magical impact of the words of power that are significant, rather than the gender of the person performing the rite. (Please read part one, chapter 8, on the assumption of the godform, to learn how to do this correctly.)

Egyptian magic works by identifying a present situation with a *Zep Tepi* (First Time) event—that is, with an event that happened in the primeval time, involving acts of the neteru. The mythical happenings of the Zep Tepi, when the deities were living on earth, thus manifest in the present. (Refer to part one, chapter 7, for more on Zep Tepi.) The

Zep Tepi event that is being evoked here is Horus's act of res-
urrecting his father Osiris and reviving him by offering him
his own Eye or inner potency—a portion of his own vitality.
As you direct the ritual implement at the statue, feel the
power of Horus in you, and direct the psychic-etheric energy
toward the mouth and eyes of the statue. Imagine that the
statue really is coming to life and that by your act its mouth
and eyes really are opened so that it becomes a vehicle for the
divine presence to enter and operate through. The statue is
no longer an inanimate object, but a vessel for the presence
of the living deity.

Now make the offerings of the incense or perfume, drink,
and food. The statue may be anointed with the water, and
the incense, if using joss sticks, may be waved in front of it.
As you make each offering, say: "O *N*, take the Eye of Horus."
(Insert the name of the deity in place of *N*.) If you have a
copy of the *Pyramid Texts*, you may like to refer to utterances
26–8, 32, 47, 54–5, 85, 87–9, 108, 110–15, 160–2, and 192 for
the correct wording of various offerings.

When this rite has been done, thank the deities you
have invoked, and dissolve the circle as usual. The incense
should be left until it has burnt, and the food and drink
should be left in front of the statue for several hours. The
ancient Egyptians believed that the spiritual essence of the
food and drink would be consumed by the deities or by
spirits of the deceased to whom such offerings were made,
and the physical food and drink could be consumed by the

priesthood later; so you can have it yourself after it has been left for a while.

The statue should now be kept very safe and treated with reverence, because the spirit of the deity inhabits it.

CHAPTER FIVE

INVOKING THE NETERU

Evocation and Invocation

Evocation and invocation are often confused, even by people who are trying to explain the differences between them, and this could lead to serious problems, because they refer to quite distinct techniques involving different kinds of entity.

Invocation is the calling of a spiritual entity into one's presence, inside a magic circle, inside a shrine, into a sacred space, or into oneself or someone else acting as a vehicle for that purpose.

Evocation is the conjuring up of an entity outside oneself, outside the magic circle, and preferably contained within a boundary traditionally called the triangle of art or triangle of conjuration.

Sometimes it is claimed that an entity may be evoked to physical appearance. Most often it is seen clairvoyantly, perhaps within a magic mirror. Entities that are invoked are also seen clairvoyantly, usually in an inner vision. However, observers can sometimes clairvoyantly see invoked entities that take control of a subject's body, manifesting either as a subtle alteration of the facial features of the subject, as a halo effect, or as a shadowy figure hovering behind the subject.

Invocation is always reserved for deities and higher spiritual entities, not for lower entities. Conversely, a deity should never be evoked, for this is to place a barrier between oneself and the evoked entity, confining it to a specified area for one's own protection. To attempt to evoke and then banish a deity would be grossly insulting, and frankly foolish. By definition, deities are mighty beings, far above us in power and holiness, and if they answer our prayers, it is through their grace, not by our bidding.

Invoking Deity

You will need a picture or statue of the deity to be invoked, a suitable prayer or invocation (such as one of those in part two of this book), a suitable incense or perfume, candles, a wand, sistrum, and other desired equipment. The image of the deity is to be placed on the shrine or altar, to help with the visualization.

Cast the magic circle and call on the elemental powers and Sons of Horus in the usual ways (Refer to part one, chapter 3). Light the candles on the altar or shrine. Light the incense (or place the perfumed oil in the evaporator and light the tea candle). Shake the sistrum. Recite the invocation. Look at the image of the deity. Close your eyes and try to visualize the deity as clearly as possible. See that image in your mind's eye coming to life and sense the deity in the circle with you. Perhaps he or she may speak or otherwise convey to you some message.

It is important that you establish from the start that the deity before you is the one that was invoked. Ask him or her, in the name of the deity who was invoked or in the name of your patron deity, to confirm his or her identity. For instance, if you invoked Isis or you are a devotee of Isis, say, "In the name of Isis, the mighty Lady, please identify yourself." As the entity has been challenged by means of a holy name, this acts as a test to ensure that it is not some mischievous spirit passing itself off as divine, because evil spirits shun the holy names. Another good form of question for a test is to ask, "Do you accept Osiris as Lord?" (use the name of your patron deity). An evil spirit will not accept divine authority, but a genuine deity will give an unambiguous reply in the affirmative because deities acknowledge one another's divinity. However, one should be aware of a deity's sensibilities and avoid offending him or her with certain names; for instance, Osiris, Isis, and Horus may not like the name of Set to be mentioned, and vice versa. When you have established that the contact is genuinely divine, ask for a sign so that you may be able to recognize this deity on other occasions. The deity may then give you a sign or secret password that you must not disclose to anyone for it is a means by which you will always be able to recognize the real deity and avoid deception from other entities. Very soon you will come to know the deity as a friend in any case, and there will be no difficulty with recognition, but these precautions are important with early contact. (Refer to part one, chapter 8, Testing Spirits.)

As you come to know the deity, he or she may give advice or disclose information to help you. It is important to be cautious about this also, as any spirit message is only as good as the medium who receives it. Sometimes a message may be ambiguous or garbled or it may be conveyed in a cryptic manner. Although deities appear to speak clearly to us in meditation, the process is actually quite similar to divination and is not absolutely reliable. This is not because the deities are deliberately deceptive, but because it can be difficult to receive the message clearly, sometimes because one may be misled by one's own wishful thinking or by preconceptions about what the deity will say. Never act on advice against your own conscience, even if it seems to come from Deity. To be on the safe side, ask for confirmation of the message on three or four occasions if you have any doubts. Write down your experiences immediately after each meditation so that you can refer to them later.

When you have invoked a deity, always give thanks to that deity at the end of the rite for help received.

CHAPTER SIX

TOTEM ANIMALS

One of the most conspicuous features of ancient Egyptian religion is the number of deities that are animals or birds. This curious concept distinguishes Egyptian religion from other forms of Paganism, but is often misunderstood, and to some extent has been the cause of Egyptian Paganism acquiring a bad reputation. Neteru that have animal and bird heads on human bodies appear sinister to some people, and worship of such beings is often associated in the popular imagination with black magic. It is erroneously supposed that a genuinely sophisticated spirituality would not involve the conceptualization of divine forces as animals and birds. It is often overlooked that even in Christianity the lamb and the dove appear as divine symbols. In a religion of an ancient civilization based on a rural culture in which people lived close to nature, it is entirely understandable that the Divine would be seen as animal and bird forms as well as humans when meditated upon.

It is likely that ancient Egyptian religion developed from a shamanic form of religion in which a shaman priest would dress as an animal or bird, enter an altered state of consciousness, and commune with spirits in the forms of animals and birds. Evidence of these practices is very apparent in Egyptian religion. The deities are often depicted as humans with the heads of animals and birds, and this may well be because the priesthood wore masks in the form of the animals and birds sacred to the various deities. It is known, for instance, that priests of Anubis wore jackal masks. Several examples of Anubis masks have survived. Religious rituals sometimes took the form of an enactment of sacred myths, and for this the priesthood would have dressed up as the deities, wearing appropriate masks.

Other aspects of shamanism are apparent in surviving religious texts. In the *Pyramid Texts*, *Coffin Texts*, and *Book of the Dead*, certain spells are to bring about the transformation of the practitioner into an animal or bird form. Egyptians may have believed such transformation to be a power acquired after death, but there is no reason to assume that the ability to shapeshift was confined to the postmortem state; in fact, there is good reason to think otherwise. Magicians and witches have always had the reputation of being shapeshifters—a belief that is found in many cultures, and ancient Egypt is no exception.

The ancient Egyptians believed in what are now called subtle bodies—nonmaterial aspects of a human being. The most important of these are the ka and the ba. As explained in part one, chapter 2, one of the meanings of the term *ka* is "double," which may correspond to the modern concept of the etheric body. The term *ba* is used to refer to the soul when it leaves the physical body, and this idea may correspond to the modern concept of the astral body, which is the form taken when one is having an out-of-body experience. However, different writers have interpreted these Egyptian terms in various ways. The etheric body is thought to be of a plastic material that can take on any form. In Egyptian magic this ability is used to take on the forms of animals as well as those of the neteru. A magician can take the form of an animal during astral projection on the physical plane and also when traveling on the inner planes or astral plane. There are two methods of doing this. While sitting quietly in meditation, one can visualize oneself as taking the form of an animal or bird. Alternatively, the form of the animal or bird may be visualized, and then one's consciousness may be projected into it. The latter technique is often more difficult, but it is the best method for using the animal form for astral projection on the physical plane. When leaving one's physical body, it is always important to work within a magic circle and ask the deities to protect one's physical body. When traveling on the inner planes, an environment should be visualized that is appropriate to the form of animal or bird that one has adopted. It may be helpful to use the genuine ancient Egyptian spells for shapeshifting, such as chapters 78, 84, 86, and 88 in the *Book of the Dead*.

Another way to work with totem animals is to call upon spirit guides in the form of animals. To do this, sit quietly in your magic circle, invoke the deities as usual, and request that they bring to you a suitable spirit animal or bird to act as your guide. Visualize the deity coming to you, bringing the animal or bird who is to act as a guide. Because it has been introduced to you by a deity on the first occasion, you know that it can be trusted (provided the proper tests have been done to establish the true identity of the deity, as described in the previous chapter and in further detail in part one, chapter 8, Testing Spirits). Now you need to establish a rapport with the spirit and find a way of identifying it on subsequent occasions. As in the case of the deities, it may give you a secret sign or password by which you will know it on future occasions. The spirit animal will often stay with you and be at hand when you call on it for help, and gradually you will find a way of communicating with it, picking up ideas from it intuitively.

CHAPTER SEVEN

EGYPTIAN MAGIC

For the ancient Egyptians, *heka* (magic) was inseparable from religious practice, and was also part of normal everyday life—from medicine and childbirth to farming and state occasions, heka was everywhere. It was conceived by a divine energy that had been with the Creator in the beginning, and by means of which he had brought about the whole of creation (*Coffin Texts*, Spell 261). As we shall see, the utterance of words of power was intrinsic to this concept of heka, and it can thus be regarded as approximating the Christian concept of the Logos or Word of God (Robert K. Ritner in Lloyd, 1992, p. 192). As the Word of God and as the first manifestation of God, Heka was personified as a god. However, as an all-pervading energy circulating in the universe, heka was sometimes associated with female powers, as implied in chapter 24 of the *Book of the Dead*, which is a spell for bringing magical power to a person in the underworld. Here we read:

> Behold, thou gatherest together the charm from every place where it is, and from every man with whom it is, swifter than greyhounds and quicker than light, the charm which created the forms of being from the mother, and which either createth the gods or maketh them to be silent, and which giveth the heat of fire unto the gods.
>
> —*Translation by E. A. Wallis Budge.*

Here we see that the magical power, heka, is a creative, life-giving energy that comes from "the mother"—a goddess or female ancestor.

The pharaoh himself was the chief magician, carrying out daily ceremonies, which were thought to keep the cosmos running harmoniously, with the power of heka. When he could not perform these rites in person, priests carried them out on his behalf in temples across the land. The king's magic made the sun rise every morning, kept the land fertile, and ensured that the Nile flooded each year, as well as warded off invasion by foreign forces.

Ordinary people had their own form of heka, which could be benign, but was sometimes distinctly black magic by modern standards, although the ancient Egyptians would not have classified it as such. The Graeco–Egyptian magical papyri from the early centuries AD contain spells in Greek and Demotic (a form of the Egyptian language), which give instructions on divination, love spells, healing, and curses. The much more ancient material of the *Pyramid Texts*, *Coffin Texts*, and *Book of the Dead* demonstrates a profoundly magical worldview.

Methods of Egyptian magic practiced by peasants, priests, and the king alike display four main principles: images, identification with the neteru, words of power, and repetition of Zep Tepi events. We shall look at these in turn.

For the Egyptians, to depict something was to bring it into being in the magical realm that we might call the astral plane, such that sooner or later it would manifest in a more tangible way. We are familiar with this idea from Voodoo: a wax image of an enemy stuck with pins is believed to bring a corresponding harm to that enemy. The Egyptians used wax images in exactly this way. An image of a dangerous animal, such as a snake or crocodile, was thought to pose a real danger, so was often represented in a mutilated form, divided in half, or with a knife through it. Images could also be beneficial: pictures of bread, cattle, and jars of beer in a tomb would ensure the deceased had enough to eat and drink in the afterlife. Supplications to the deities were often written on tablets adorned with pictures of ears to ensure that the prayers would be heard. Eyes were painted on the sides of coffins so that the dead would be able to look out. An image could never be just an inert representation; in a real sense it became the object that it represented and had the power to bring about any situation depicted.

Identification with the deities was an important aspect of Egyptian magic. In the past, Egyptologists construed it as "boasting" when they came across texts in which a king or deceased person claimed to be a god or equal to the gods. There is a sense, however, in which this was the reverse of boasting, for it was recognized that the human individual, even a magician, might not have the power to bring about the desired magical effect. It was only by total identification with a god or goddess, by becoming that neter and thereby channeling the power of that neter, that the magical forces required could be generated.

Words of power were a vital aspect of magic for the Egyptians. These words were chiefly the names of the deities. To know the true name of a thing, animal, person, deity, or demon was to have power over that being. In the *Book of the Dead*, the deceased person passes through the underworld safely by knowing the correct names of the gates, their guardians, and other entities and objects encountered. A famous spell to cure a snake bite, known as the Legend of Ra and Isis, describes how Isis tricks Ra into revealing his secret name to her, whereupon she takes his power to govern the universe for herself and her son Horus. The later Graeco–Egyptian magical papyri are dominated by long lists of words of power, which are plainly deity names that have become garbled over decades or even centuries of repetition and copying. In fact, the correct pronunciation and intonation of names and words of power was essential. A deceased person was said to be "true of voice," which did not just mean truthful, but meant having a knowledge of the correct words and the correct pronunciation to be able to placate the gods and demons of the underworld and so survive in the afterlife. This is something of a problem for us today, since we do not know the correct pronunciation of the ancient Egyptian language, which was written without vowels. We have to do the best we can with the surviving spells, used in translation. This is generally considered to be adequate, as magical intention is at least as important as the words.

It is also possible to construct one's own spells if the principle is understood. The Egyptians based their magic on events that happened in the mythical primeval time called the Zep Tepi, and these events involved the actions of the neteru. The Egyptian magician would identify a Zep Tepi event corresponding to the situation on which he intended his spell to operate, and then constructed a spell so that the outcome would be the same as what happened in the Zep Tepi. For example, Horus, while in hiding as a child, fell ill on several occasions and was healed by his mother Isis. To perform a healing spell, the magician tells the patient a story about Isis healing Horus. He puts the patient in the role of Horus and himself in the role of Isis and, speaking the words of Isis as she healed Horus, heals the patient. As Horus was healed by his mother Isis, so will the patient be healed. Other actions may be involved, such as the administering of a herbal remedy or the making of a talisman.

The method for working a spell is as follows. First, identify a relevant Zep Tepi event using genuine Egyptian texts if possible. In some of E. A. Wallis Budge's books, the actual texts are reproduced in hieroglyphs with a transliteration into the Roman alphabet and a translation into English, which is ideal for this purpose. Gather together the materials that will be needed, such as paper, pen, and ink for drawing a talisman; suitable incense and colored candles for the deities invoked and the type of spell; statues of deities; and any other item needed, such as an amulet or wax image. (A wax image is not used only for curses, but in certain cases of absent healing and other spells, too.) Write down the wording of the rite you are going to use, so that you will not forget what you are doing. Cast the circle in the usual way and invoke the relevant deities. Referring to your script, tell the story of the appropriate Zep Tepi event, identifying yourself with the god or goddess involved, and "ground" the energy of the spell in the talisman, amulet, or wax image. Thank the deities, close down the circle, and keep the talisman, amulet, or image in a safe place.

This sounds simple, but in fact involves a great deal of preparation. A familiarity with Egyptian myths is important. Here are some situations in the Zep Tepi that could be employed in spells.

Healing: Isis heals Horus

Defeat an enemy: Horus defeats Set, or Ra defeats
Apep

Calm a person or situation: Pacification of Sekhmet

Return an unfaithful lover: Isis's love for Osiris despite
his affair with Nephthys

Protection: Neteru protect Osiris

Relieve depression: Hathor exposes herself to Ra

Conceive a child: Isis conceives Horus

Find a lost thing: Anubis finds parts of Osiris's body

Happy marriage: Hathor and Horus

Creativity: Khepera creates the world

There are, however, two important matters to be taken into account when performing a spell. The first is whether the spell is ethical. Although ancient Egyptian magicians were not averse to laying curses and using extreme forms of psychological manipulation, most modern magicians and Pagans would advise against such an approach. For instance, the second example above, a spell to defeat an enemy, would be appropriate for overcoming a negative habit in oneself, such as smoking; but to use such a spell against another individual, to do that person harm, might be justifiable, if at all, only in the most extreme circumstances. In such a case, it would be best to emphasize that the dispute between Horus and Set was eventually resolved justly through the advocacy of Thoth in a tribunal of the gods. To use magic to return an unfaithful lover or to secure a happy marriage might also be considered unethical if this involves interfering with another person's free will. To use magic to cause a particular individual to fall in love with oneself or to attempt matchmaking on behalf of others, is morally questionable. A spell to return an unfaithful lover should concentrate on healing the relationship involving oneself, rather than splitting up the other relationship. If seeking a sexual partner or suitable spouse, it is best to work toward finding any suitable person, rather than naming a specific individual who may not want such a relationship. Even a healing spell could be unethical if the sick person has not given permission for magic to be performed on his or her behalf, especially if that person is opposed to magic on religious or ideological grounds.

The second point to be taken into consideration is how to word the spell for the best result. Care should be taken that the wording is not ambiguous, and also that one is not working toward making the situation worse. For example, someone might carelessly perform a spell to have a relationship like that of Isis and Osiris, neglecting to mention that it is love and faithfulness that is wanted, rather than widowhood at a young age. It is important to anticipate what might go wrong with a spell in order to avoid problems, and resort to magic only when other more mundane methods have been tried first.

To perform spells, which is sometimes called Low Magic (magic for a practical or material end), is not the main subject in this book, which concentrates on High Magic (spiritual enhancement and communion with Deity), but we have provided this information here so that you will understand the basic principles and in case you wish to investigate this area further yourself. A very good book on how to work Egyptian magic is, *Ancient Egyptian Divination and Magic*, by Eleanor L. Harris.

CHAPTER EIGHT

ASSUMPTION OF THE GODFORM

The technique we are going to describe here is often known as channeling. In the Bible, it is called "prophesying" (which does not necessarily imply predicting the future) and is defined in Christian terms as one of the gifts of the Holy Spirit. Witches call it "drawing down the moon" (when it is performed on a woman) and "drawing down the sun" (when performed on a man). As already explained, assumption of the godform was practiced widely by the ancient Egyptian priesthood, who would dress as the neteru and wear animal masks while playing the parts of divine characters in sacred dramas. As explained earlier, the practice was also central to the working of Low Magic, in which the practitioners identified with the deities while uttering words of power, so that divine energies would be channeled through them to bring about the desired magical effect.

In High Magic, the assumption of the godform is performed so as to receive spiritual guidance or purely for the experience of communion with the Divine. During this practice, the subject purportedly allows a discarnate entity to occupy his or her body in order to deliver a spiritual message or to perform a particular magical function in a ritual. This occurs when the subject is either in a state of trance, has temporarily left the body, or has allowed the entity to overshadow his or her personal will. Someone in this state of consciousness will speak and act as the occupying entity.

There are various ways of interpreting this. Skeptics may dismiss the phenomenon as simply role-playing and fantasizing; but for a magician, fantasy and role-play are valuable psychological techniques, so to attempt to discredit such a method is irrelevant from the magician's point of view. Some people may not believe in discarnate entities, but would explain the phenomenon in terms of unconscious processes and archetypes of the collective unconscious. Most people who think this, however, tend to believe in the objective reality of the entities they are temporarily manifesting, not only because of the subjective experience, being taken over by a separate entity, but because behaving as if this is reality also achieves the best results.

It is important that the technique be used only for channeling higher spiritual entities, and not demons, evil spirits, or unidentified entities. Even if one believes that they are only aspects of one's own unconscious mind, it is still very dangerous to allow such negative forces to dominate the psyche, even for short periods of time. After the occupying entity has departed, its influence may be around for a long time afterward. If this is a good influence of a higher spiritual nature, it will be uplifting and enhance one's life. If it is a bad influence, which stimulates one's worst impulses, then it will drag one down with it.

Visualizing the Godform

A godform is the form that a particular deity takes. Distinctive appearance, style of dress, and symbolism identify the godform of a particular deity. This does not mean that the deity really does have a body with that appearance—it is merely a conventional appearance to represent deities that may be adopted by them in order to reveal themselves to us in visions. Some deities, however, have more than one godform, including their totem animals.

A godform may be regarded as a construction on the astral plane, which is then ensouled by a deity. When performing the assumption of the godform, one must first visualize the godform very clearly while invoking the deity to whom it belongs. The deity should then ensoul the godform and appear in one's mind's eye as a living, moving being.

When assuming the godform, it may help to adopt the characteristic pose of the godform you are going to assume, and in a ritual situation you may even dress as the deity and hold appropriate symbols and implements.

Gender and Godforms

It is possible to assume a godform of a different gender to one's own. In some circumstances, however, this may be quite inappropriate; for instance, in a group when a priest-ess is present, it would be very peculiar for a priest or male member of the group to assume the godform of a goddess, since this is the role of the priestess.

There are, however, some occasions when it may be appropriate: if one is working alone or in a group where no one of the same gender as the deity is present. It is also appropriate in Low Magic uses of the technique. Women can identify with the God through the animus, and men can identify with the Goddess through the anima, to use Jungian terminology. The anima or animus is an archetypal figure that personifies the unconscious mind, and is female for a man and male for a woman.

Testing the Spirits

As explained in the chapter on invocation, mischievous spirits are repelled by holy names and will not acknowledge Deity, and all deities acknowledge one another. It is best to test a spirit in the name of the deity that you venerate. Also, it is best for this purpose not to use the name of a deity associated with chaos, darkness, or destruction that has an ambiguous nature—not because such deities are evil in themselves (there is no such thing as an evil deity), but because they are beyond good and evil, morally neutral, and may tolerate evil spirits to the extent that their services may occasionally be commissioned for a higher purpose. Evil spirits may be less likely to be repelled by the names of Set and Sekhmet, who sometimes have demons in their service, than by the names of Isis and Ra. A few neteru, of which Set is a notable example, are unsuitable for invocation and assumption of the godform by beginners, although experienced practitioners would have no problems with them.

When you have invoked a deity and you clairvoyantly see an entity approaching, challenge it politely but authoritatively in the name of the deity that you venerate. Be respectful, because in all likelihood this is the deity that you have invoked. If it is the deity in whose name you utter the challenge, it will confirm this. If it is another deity, he or she will acknowledge the one you have named, before giving his or her own name. You should then ask how you will recognize this deity in the future, and the deity will show you a special symbol or sign or otherwise explain how he or she may be recognized. Egyptian deities are often more readily identifiable than those of other cultures because they have animal or bird heads or have distinctive headdresses.

If you are not satisfied that this really is the deity that he or she claims to be, or if the spirit answers ambiguously and avoids giving direct answers, explain your misgivings and ask the spirit politely, in the name of the deity you venerate, to depart. If it was a deity after all, and not a deceptive spirit, the deity will understand why you are taking such precautions and will not be offended, but will bless you and leave peacefully. If the entity argues back, criticizes your precautions, and is reluctant to leave, this only goes to prove that your misgivings were entirely justified. This is unlikely to happen, however, because when deities are invoked sincerely, they invariably come, and evil spirits are banished by the divine presence. The test described here is merely a safeguard, but it is an important one, because you are going to invite the entity to inhabit your body. If you should ever experience a troublesome entity, especially if it is reluctant to leave, open your eyes to stop the visualization of the entity. Call upon the deity whom you venerate, and politely request that he or she escort the entity from the circle and provide you with protection. Imagine that this is happening and believe that it is so. Visualize a protective blue light around you, and thank your deity for the help received. If you ever feel the need for psychic protection when outside the circle, imagine that you are wearing a long, blue, hooded cloak.

Assuming the Godform

When you are satisfied that the entity you can see clairvoyantly is indeed the deity you have invoked, visualize the figure standing directly in front of you, life size. Very often, when one first visualizes a godform or indeed any image, it may seem quite small and appear as if it is at the other end of a tunnel. This is a common experience of clairvoyant vision, and indeed people are sometimes taught to develop the third eye by imagining that they are looking down a tube. If you have this experience, it will be necessary to enlarge the image. You must very clearly imagine that the deity is in the room with you, just as surely as if someone were standing in that position before you. Try to be aware of the presence of the deity in as full a sense as possible.

Tell the deity that you wish to assume the godform, and then visualize the figure walking around your chair and stopping behind you. (Alternatively, he or she may turn around and step backwards into you, but this is not the recommended method. If you are standing up, you may step forward to enter the godform from behind, but this is not recommended for the beginner, who is advised to remain seated while in a trance.) The deity, from behind you, steps forward and enters your body. The focus for this blending is the nape of the neck; you may sense the divine energy pouring in at this point as you assume the godform. If this is done correctly, you will feel as if you are inside the godform and that it has enveloped you.

From now until the deity departs, your personal consciousness will retreat and the divine personality will dominate your consciousness. It is best to remain seated with your eyes closed during this process. With experience, it may become possible to open your eyes, stand up, and move about as the neter or *neteret* (goddess) whose form you have assumed, but this is difficult.

Delivering an Oracle

While you are assuming the godform, you will think and feel as the neter or neteret whose form you have assumed. Words that you would like to speak aloud may come to mind, and if this happens you should allow the utterances to come spontaneously and not analyze or censor them in any way. As it says in the Bible, "For prophesy never had its origin in the will of man, but men spoke from God, as they were carried along by the Holy Spirit" (2 Peter 1:21).

Sometimes such utterances will seem meaningless, cryptic, or even gibberish, and often they are couched in weird metaphors or similes; but if one tries to censor or control this while in the altered state of consciousness, the contact is likely to be broken immediately and the deity will depart. Therefore, any reservations that one may have should be put aside until later. It may be helpful to use a tape recorder to record any channeled messages, so that they can be reviewed afterward.

In part two of this book, some of the invocations are followed by replies from the deities. It may be helpful to read the reply before assuming the godform of that deity. If the deity is going to be invoked regularly, the words of the reply could be memorized and recited before the assumption of the godform takes place, to put one into the right mood before allowing the spontaneous oracle to flow on immediately afterward.

Closing Down

When the session is over, allow the deity to leave your body. To do this, visualize the spiritual essence flowing out through your solar plexus. You may, with clairvoyant vision, see it emerging like a cloud of bluish-white vapor and building up into the godform in front of you. Try to see the godform as clearly as possible, and make sure that all the spiritual essence of the deity has left your body. Always remember to thank the deity afterward; it will then bless you and depart.

A Warning about Oracles

As mentioned in part one, chapter 5, one needs to be cautious about any messages received from spirits, including deities. One should be careful about accepting such messages unquestioningly, as they are only as reliable as the channeler through whom they are delivered. Even if a genuine message is received from Deity, it may be garbled in the process of being transmitted. Also, one's personal consciousness may interfere and deliver a message distorted by wishful thinking, or impulses from the personal unconscious may distort the message.

Even if the wording seems absolutely clear and unambiguous, this in itself can be misleading, giving the impression that there is a direct channel through to Deity. Unless one is a very gifted or experienced mystic or magical adept, and such people are exceedingly rare, direct channeling is far from being the case. Channeled messages are in fact much more like divination than they at first appear. Just as a Tarot card reading, for instance, requires much caution and intuition in its interpretation, so does a channeled message. The metaphors and similes that are typical of such a message are like the pictures on the cards in a Tarot reading.

Before acting on any channeled message, therefore, it is important to consider it in the light of any other information that you may have on the issue in question. One should never act on such a message if the advice given is contrary to one's moral principles, or if it seems irrational, dangerous, or against common sense and one's better judgment. Channeled messages from spirits, especially from Deity, should be a guide and inspiration, reinforcing one's well-being and faith in Deity. Any message that seems contrary to this is best ignored, for it is safe to assume the message must have been distorted in the transmission.

It would also be very unwise for anyone who has a mental illness such as schizophrenia to perform this technique. People who have a mental illness that causes them to hear voices or see omens and portents in ordinary events are sometimes attracted to the paranormal and occult because it may seem to explain their own experience, but for such a person to engage in any sort of psychic development practice, especially this one, is risky, as it is possible that it could aggravate an existing condition.

PART TWO

A NOTE ON THE
SACRED TEXTS

In part two of this book, each chapter on the deities begins
with an extract, or several extracts, from the sacred texts of
the ancient Egyptians. We have placed these passages under
the headings Invocation, Reply, and Closing, to indicate
how the scriptures may be used by a modern Pagan in devotional practices; but this is not necessarily indicative of how
the ancient Egyptians themselves would have used them. It
may be noticed that not every chapter contains a Reply or
Closing passage, which may seem puzzling. This is not a
mistake; we used material that is currently available in

translation, gleaned from a number of books, with an aim to bring together here in one book a selection of material that could form the basis of a liturgy for modern followers of Egyptian Paganism. We were not able to find material suitable to place under all these headings for each of the deities featured.

Texts that we have designated as invocations are suitable for welcoming a deity to one's presence and will set the mood and atmosphere for beginning a rite or meditation concentrating on a particular deity. If you wish to invoke more than one deity, then more than one invocation may be used.

The passages in which we have provided a reply from the deity may be used for the same purpose as the Charge in Wiccan rites; that is, to be spoken by a priest or priestess who is assuming the godform. As already explained in part one, this is done to directly channel and receive psychic energy or a message from the deity concerned. A formal Charge or "reply," as we have called it here, is not necessary in the ideal situation where the channeling is successful. However, it is a good idea in any ritual involving group participants for the priest or priestess to have memorized a text such as this as a standby, because it may be awkward if the anticipated channeled message does not come through. It may also be helpful for a priest or priestess in a group ritual, or a solitary devotee in a meditation session, to initiate a channeling by reciting a memorized text, which may inspire a spontaneous message to follow.

The texts that we have designated as closing passages may be suitable for ending a rite or meditation. However, these are only suggestions, and if you wish to use a closing prayer as an invocation, you are free to do so! Our intention is that this material can be used in any way you may choose—incorporated into your own rites and meditations, and augmented with invocations, prayers, or other material of your own composition or from other sources.

ONE

RA-ATUM

Invocation

Homage to thee, O thou who art Ra when thou risest and Temu when thou settest. Thou risest, thou risest, thou shinest, thou shinest, thou who art crowned king of the gods. Thou art the lord of heaven, thou art the lord of earth; thou art the creator of those who dwell in the heights and those who dwell in the depths. Thou art the God One who came into being in the beginning of time. Thou didst create the earth, thou didst fashion man, thou didst make the watery abyss of the sky, thou didst form Hapi, thou didst create the watery abyss, and thou dost give life unto

all that therein is. Thou hast knit together the mountains, thou hast made mankind and the beasts of the field to come into being, thou hast made the heavens and the earth. Worshipped be thou whom the goddess Maat embraceth at morn and at eve. Thou dost travel across the sky with heart swelling with joy; the Lake of Testes becometh contented thereat. The serpent-fiend Nak hath fallen and his two arms are cut off. The Sektet boat receiveth fair winds, and the heart of him that is in the shrine thereof rejoiceth. Thou art crowned Prince of heaven, thou art the One dowered with all sovereignty who comest forth from the sky. Ra is victorious! O thou divine youth, thou heir of everlasting-ness, thou self-begotten one, O thou who didst give thyself birth! O One, mighty one, of myriad forms and aspects, king of the world, Prince of Annu, lord of eternity and ruler of everlastingness, the company of the gods rejoice when thou risest and when thou sailest across the sky, O thou who art exalted in the Sektet boat.

Homage to thee, O Amen-Ra, who dost rest upon Maat, and who passest over heaven, every face seeth thee. Thou dost wax great as thy Majesty doth advance, and thy rays are upon all faces. Thou art unknown and no tongue is worthy to declare thy likeness; only thou thyself canst do this. . . . Men praise thee in thy name Ra, and they swear by thee, for thou art lord over them. Thou hearest with thine ears and thou seest with thine eyes. Millions of years have gone over the world; I cannot tell the number of those through which thou hast passed. Thy heart hath decreed a day of happiness in thy name of "Traveller." Thou dost pass over and dost travel through untold spaces requiring millions and hundreds of thousands of years to pass over; thou passest through them in peace, and thou steerest thy way across the watery abyss to the place which thou lovest; this thou doest in one little moment of time, and then thou dost sink down and dost make an end of the hours.

—*Papyrus of Hu-nefer, translation by E. A. Wallis Budge, in* Book of the Dead, *pp. 12–15.*

Reply

The words of Neb-er-tcher which he spoke after he came
into being. I am he who came into being as Khepera. I became the creator of what came into being ... coming forth
from my mouth. Heaven existed not; earth existed not; nor
had been created the things of the earth and creeping
things in that place. I raised them up from Nu, from an
inert state. I could not find a place to stand in. I performed
a spell on my heart; I laid a foundation in Maa; I made
every form. I was alone: I had not spat out Shu, I had not
emitted Tefnut. No other existed who worked with me.

I made a foundation in my own heart. There came into
being multitudes of things which came into being of things
which came into being from things which came into being
of births from things which came into being of their births.
I, even I, had union with my fist; I united with my shadow;
I poured seed into my own mouth. I produced issue in the
form of Shu; I produced moisture in the form of Tefnut.
Said my father Nu, they make weak my Eye which is behind
them, because for double henti periods they proceeded
from me, after I became from one god three gods—that is,
from myself I came into being on this earth. Raised up,
therefore, were Shu and Tefnut in the inert watery mass in
which they were. They brought to me my Eye in their following. After, therefore, I had united my members, I wept
over them. Came into being men and women from the
tears which came forth from my Eye. It raged against me
after it came and found I had made another in its place: I

endowed it with the power I had made. Having approached, therefore, its place in my face, afterwards, therefore, it rules this earth in its entirety.

The seasons fall upon their plants. I endowed it with what it has taken possession of in it. I came forth as the plants, all creeping things, things which came into being— in them all. Shu and Tefnut give birth to Geb and Nut. Geb and Nut give birth to Osiris, Horus-Khent-an-maati, Set, Isis, Nephthys, from the womb, one after another of them: they give birth; they multiply on this earth.

—*Papyrus number 10, 188 in the British Museum, based on the transliteration by E. A. Wallis Budge, in* The Gods of the Egyptians, *Volume I, pp. 308–13.*

Closing

Hail to you, O Ra, in your life and in your beauty, in your thrones, in your [gold]. Bring me the milk of Isis, the flood of Nephthys, the overspill of the lake, the surge of the sea, life, prosperity, health, happiness, bread, beer, clothing, and food, that I may live thereby. . . . May I see you when you go forth as Thoth, when a waterway is prepared for the bark of Ra to his fields which are in Iasu; may you rush on as one who is at the head of his Chaos-gods.

—*Pyramid Texts, utterance 406, translation by R. O. Faulkner, reprinted by permission of Oxford University Press.*

Ra is the sun god, the Creator, whose main cult center was at Heliopolis (the Greek name for Annu, Iunu, or On), situated in what is now the outskirts of Cairo. There he was identified with an older deity called Atum, to become Atum-Ra or Ra-Atum. The name Atum is generally taken to mean "all" or "completeness," but paradoxically it could also mean "nothingness" or "he who is not yet present." Atum, also called Tem or Temu, originally a creator god, came to be seen as the aspect of the solar creator associated with the setting sun. Ra is usually represented as a falcon or a man with a falcon's head, wearing a solar disc. Atum may be represented as an old man leaning on his staff or as a king wearing the combined crowns of Upper and Lower Egypt. The Heliopolitan theology was one of the chief forms of the religion of ancient Egypt and was closely associated with the cult of the pharaoh.

The hymn that we have used here for the invocation reveals a number of beliefs about Ra: that he is the Creator of all that exists, the Supreme Being (God One, that is, the only Deity), and that he has a solar form and is conceptualized as traveling over the heavens in a boat. Reference is made here to the goddess Maat, who represents order, justice, and truth; and to the serpent-fiend Nak (otherwise called Apep or Apophis), who represents the forces of chaos that must be defeated each day as Ra maintains his creation. It was believed that various gods and goddesses assisted him in this struggle against the "serpent of chaos." This hymn also identifies Ra with Amun, the hidden god. Hapi, another god mentioned, is the deity presiding over the Nile.

The passage we have chosen for Ra-Atum's reply is taken from a much longer text describing the battle against Apep and was used in magical rites to defeat the forces of chaos. In the section we have used, Ra, called here Neb-er-tcher (the Lord of All), describes his first act of creation, by which the Ennead is formed and everything else is generated. The Ennead (the Greek term for the Egyptian word *pesedjet*, meaning "nine") is a group of nine deities, although the word tends to be used quite loosely for a company of gods and goddesses comprised of more or less than nine. The nine deities forming the Heliopolitan Ennead are: Ra-Atum himself, Shu, Tefnut, Geb, Nut, Osiris, Set, Isis, and Nephthys. In the the text chosen for the god's reply above, a form of Horus the Elder is also included. (As we shall explain in later chapters, there were various forms of Horus.) Ra-Atum, it says here, came into being as Khepera, whose name means "the one who comes into being," and this form of the Deity is represented as a scarab beetle, a creature thought to be generated spontaneously out of dead matter—a misunderstanding of its habit of laying its eggs in dung.

This text is important for a proper understanding of ancient Egyptian religious beliefs. It is made very clear here that everything is generated from the one Deity. The act of creation is described in sexual terms, and in the past some commentators have regarded this account as, at best, unsophisticated, at worst, as crude and improper; but this only demonstrates the pitfalls of interpreting religious, mystical, and poetic writings too literally. What is suggested here is rather that a very simple, humble, self-pleasuring act by the Creator initiates a process that brings the whole universe into being. He starts by performing a spell on his heart, the essence of his being and the center of thinking and conscience according to the Egyptians, and he establishes a foundation in Maa, which is the principle of order, truth, and justice personified by Maat—which is to say, everything that follows is done in this context of rightness and the divinely established order. This foundation of Maat is represented in pictures as a small platform with a sloping front on which a god stands, and is the hieroglyph for the sound "maa." Ra-Atum's two children, Shu, the god of air, and Tefnut, the goddess of moisture, are formed of his own bodily substance, his spittle, and are therefore emanations of himself. These three deities comprise a triad or threefold Deity—a concept which may well have influenced the Christian idea of the Trinity. (We address this idea in more detail in later chapters on Shu and Maat.)

What happens next, although described fairly vaguely in this version of the story, is known from elsewhere in this document and from other sources. Shu and Tefnut, with their father, are standing on the primeval mound that has risen out of the waters of Nun or Nu. Nu appears in this text as a god in his own right, but there is a sense in which he was not a god until Ra-Atum had differentiated himself from Nu as a self-conscious Being. Nu or the Nun is conceived of as an inert watery mass that existed before creation. The primeval mound, here described as the foundation made in Maa, is elsewhere identified with the Benben Stone or pyramidion (the summit of a pyramid). Shu and Tefnut slip off the primeval mound into the water and are swept away. Ra-Atum plucks out his own eye and sends it in search of them. The Eye takes the form of a goddess identified with Hathor, Sekhmet, and some other goddesses. When she returns with the lost children, she finds that Ra has grown a replacement eye and she can never again resume her position in his face. Ra weeps for joy at being reunited with his children and his tears become human beings. Other texts indicate that it is the disembodied Eye that weeps, the one that has become a goddess, and hers are not tears of joy but of grief and rage at her father's apparent rejection of her. Ra-Atum placates her by placing her on his brow in the form of a sacred serpent or uraeus, his third eye, which is also his symbol of power and protection. However, the damage has already been done. What started as something small, intimate, and pleasurable, with every good intention, has developed into a situation of separation, suffering, grief, anger, and misunderstanding, and human beings are formed from the resulting tears.

This association between humans and tears is based on the fact that the Egyptian words for these concepts sound similar, and for the Egyptians this would have indicated a deep affinity between the two concepts. In *Conception of God in Ancient Egypt*, Erik Hornung explains that this story points to the intrinsic "blindness" of human beings: we are formed from the tears that temporarily blinded the Deity, but for us that "blindness" is a permanent condition, for Ra-Atum's blinding tears are the very essence of our being. As Hornung observes:

> God overcame the affliction of his eye, but man's origin means that he is destined never to partake in the clear sight of god; affliction blights everything he sees, thinks, and does. How painfully this image from an early civilization and from the depths of man's soul brings home to us the inadequacy of even the most exact theory of origin. (1996, p. 150)

His remarks also show why scientific explanations can never be a substitute for myth: the "exact theory" provided by science is only one way of seeing. Myth should never be viewed as a primitive sort of pseudoscience, for it operates quite differently, using symbolism to reveal spiritual truths that touch us on an emotional level. As we shall see in later chapters, the ancient Egyptians sought, through their religion, salvation from spiritual blindness by finding a way back to godhead and identification with the Divine. This is the basis of our true nature, as the myth explains.

Many people have a concept of God as a remote and domineering being, dispassionately ordering his creation, responsible for the ills of the world but not himself suffering as a consequence. This ancient Egyptian myth presents a very different picture. Here is a Deity who is bound up with his creation in the most intimate and personal way. He masturbates, experiences orgasm, loves his children; he suffers loss, pain, and mutilation, but also experiences healing and the joy of reunion. His emotions spill out in tears. Although he is basically male, his Eye is female, and his hand with which he unites sexually was also thought of by the Egyptians as the feminine aspect of the Deity. His children, emanations of himself, are male and female. Everything we experience in the world is described here as being present at the beginning: it is all potentially present within the one Deity, and he generates everything out of his own being, because everything that comes into being is the coming into being of "the one who comes into being," Khepera. Ra-Atum says here that he is in everything—the other gods, the plants, the creatures. Everything is brought into being through the agency of the other gods of the Ennead who comprise heaven and Earth and what we call the forces of nature. It is important to understand, however, that these other deities are not really to be thought of as individual deities, for they are all emanations of the one Deity and are all aspects of him or her. Human beings and all plants and animals are also all manifestations of this one Divine Being. Although this Deity is immanent (within the material world), he or she still retains a transcendent aspect and is not totally subsumed within nature. The whole of creation is a divine emanation; each god and goddess is a form of the one God; every person and creature contains the divine spark; but beyond all this, the Supreme Being still retains his or her original nature as the Supreme Being.

TWO

AMUN

Invocation

Praisegiving to Amun.
I make for him adorations to his name,
I give him praises to the height of heaven,
And over the breadth of the earth,
I tell his might to travelers north and south:
Beware ye of him!
Declare him to son and daughter,
    To the great and small,
Herald him to generations,
    Not yet born;

Herald him to fishes in the deep,
  To birds in the sky,
Declare him to fool and wise,
Beware ye of him!

You are Amun, the Lord of the silent,
Who comes at the voice of the poor;
When I call to you in my distress,
You come to rescue me,
To give breath to him who is wretched,
To rescue me from bondage.

You are Amen-Ra, Lord of Thebes,
Who rescues him who is in [duat];
For you are he who is merciful,
When one appeals to you,
      You are he who comes from afar.

—*Votive Stela of Nebre, from Deir el-Medina, Berlin Museum 20377,*
   in Ancient Egyptian Literature, *Volume II, by Miriam Lichtheim,*
   pp. 105–6.

Reply

Words spoken by him whose names are secret, the Lord of All, who said to the Silent Ones who raged when the Entourage sailed: Go in peace! I will relate to you the two good deeds which my own heart did for me within the Coiled One in order that falsehood might be silenced. I have done four good deeds within the portal of the horizon. I made the four winds that everyone might breathe in his time. Such was my deed in the matter. I made a great flood so that the poor as well as the great might be strong. Such was my deed in the matter. I made every man equal to his fellow, and I forbade them to do wrong, but their hearts disobeyed what I had said. Such was my deed in the matter. I made their hearts not to forget the West, in order to make god's offerings to the gods of the nomes. Such was my deed in the matter.

I created the gods from my sweat, and mankind from the tears of my eye; I will shine anew daily in their booth for the Lord of All, I made night for Him who was languid. I will navigate aright in my bark, for I am the Lord of waters when crossing the sky, I am not rejected because of any member of mine. Hu is in company with Magic, felling yonder Ill-disposed One for me, I see the horizon, I sit before it, I judge between the wretched and the wealthy; so also as regards the evildoers. I possess life because I am its lord, and my staff will not be taken away. I have passed myriads of years between myself and yonder Inert One, the son of Geb; I will sit with him in the one place, and mounds will be towns and towns will be mounds; mansion will desolate mansion.

I am the lord of fire who lives by truth, lord of eternity, who creates joy, and the snakes of aftet will not rebel against me . . .

—Coffin Texts, *spell 1130, translation by R. O. Faulkner.*

Closing

But One alone is the hidden God, who hides himself
  from them all,
    who conceals himself from gods, whose features cannot be known.
He is farther above than heaven, deeper down than the
  world below
    and no gods at all can know his true nature.
No picture of him blossoms forth in the writings;
    there is no witness concerning him,
He is mysterious to the depths of his majesty—
    great beyond any perception of him,
      mighty beyond comprehension.

> An enemy dead on the instant in terror is he who
>   mentions God's secret Name, with intention or not.
> No god can know him by means of it—
>   God is a Spirit, hidden his Name and his Mystery.

> —*Leiden Hymn, Papyrus Leiden 1350 recto, translation by John L. Foster, in* Hymns, Prayers, and Songs: An Anthology of Ancient Egyptian Lyric Poetry, *p. 77.*

Amun (Amen or Amon) is perhaps the most transcendent concept that the ancient Egyptians had of the Supreme Being. His name means "the hidden one," and signifies the mysterious, unseen, ineffable aspect of Deity, although symbolically he was often represented as a man with a ram's head.

One only has to read the text that we have chosen for the closing passages to realize that the followers of ancient Egyptian Paganism were capable of a spiritual mode of thinking about the transcendent, ineffable nature of Deity every bit as sophisticated as that found within the monotheistic religions that developed later. At Hermopolis (called Khemnu by the Egyptians, meaning "eight-town"), Amun was one of the eight deities (Ogdoad) of primeval chaos who took the form of frogs and snakes. These deities comprise four pairs: Nun and his female counterpart Naunet, representing the primeval waters; Huh and his female counterpart Hauhet, representing infinite space or boundlessness; Kuk and his female counterpart Kauket, representing darkness; and Amun and his female counterpart Amaunet, representing all that is hidden.

Amun's main cult center was at Luxor (called Thebes by the Greeks, and Waset by the ancient Egyptians), the capital of the fourth nome (district) of Upper Egypt. During the Eighteenth Dynasty, Amun's cult came to prominence and Thebes became the capital of Egypt. Here he was worshipped as a member of a triad with his consort, the lioness or vulture mother goddess, Mut, and their son Khonsu, the moon god. Amun's great temple at Karnak, in northeastern Luxor, which was called Ipet-Isut by the ancient Egyptians, is one of the most impressive of Egyptian monuments, estimated to have had 86,000 staff when in use (Evans, 2000, pp. 56–7).

Amun became associated with Ra, as Amen-Ra, and shares many attributes with Ra and Atum, as he may be regarded as an alternative concept of the Supreme Being with an emphasis on slightly different aspects. The text we have used for Amun's reply is intended to be about Atum, but descriptions within it could equally apply to Amun-Ra, so we consider it appropriate to include here. There is reference to the god's solar attribute of traveling across the sky in a boat, protected from the Ill-disposed One (the chaos serpent) by other gods. The gods providing this protection are Hu, the personification of the authority of a word of command, and Heka (Magic), the personification of magic. These may be regarded as powers inherent in the Creator himself. These concepts of Hu and Heka have come down to us through classical religious philosophy into Christianity as the Logos (Word of God) incarnated in Jesus Christ.

We shall return to this idea in later chapters on Ptah and Thoth.

Amun was believed to have particular compassion for the poor and disadvantaged, as can be seen in the text we have chosen for the invocation. Here we see that he responds to those who call on him in distress, that he is merciful and has concern for justice and fairness, and that he helps those in the duat. The duat is the realm of the dead and the place where the sun goes at night, conceived of as the underworld or a hidden realm inside the body of the sky goddess, Nut, with the entrance and exit at the western and eastern horizons.

In the text that has been used for the god's reply, again we see the particular importance the Lord of All, whether he be Amun-Ra or Ra-Atum, places on what is right and just. These principles, he explains, were instituted by him in the "four good deeds" that he performed when he created the world. This may be taken as an alternative way of saying that the Creator made his foundation in Maat. The injustice and inequality we experience in this life were not part of the original Divine plan, for the Lord of All explains here that he made human beings equal to one another and forbade wrongdoing, but was disobeyed in this respect. Humans are formed from his tears, as explained in the previous chapter on Ra-Atum, but here the gods are created from his sweat rather than his saliva. The Egyptians regarded the sweat of a god as a perfume he gave off on account of his divine nature and by which the divine presence might be recognized (Hornung, 1982, pp. 149–50). When the god says that he made human hearts not to forget the west, he is referring to the Egyptian tradition of honoring the ancestors (for the west, the place of the setting sun, was regarded as the domain of the dead), and this practice is mentioned here in the context of general religious devotions to the gods.

A reference is made to the Coiled One, a primeval serpent, sometimes called Kematef, meaning "he who has completed his time." Amun was identified with Kematef, but this is not to be confused with Amun's direct title, Kamutef, meaning "bull of his mother." For the Egyptians, the serpent concept evoked associations with immortality and perpetual renewal because the snake is able to "renew" itself by shedding its skin. The symbol of the ouroboros, a serpent swallowing its own tail, which signifies eternity (perpetual cycles of renewal), originated with the ancient Egyptians. They called it Sito, the primeval serpent on the edge of the world, surrounding all of creation and comprising the boundary between the divinely ordered realm created by Deity, and the primordial conditions before the world came into being. For the Egyptians, the snake was an important sacred symbol, usually representing good rather than evil powers. In this particular text, it provides an alternative image for the creation of the world, which we may contrast with Atum's orgasm and subsequent evolutions as Khepera into myriads of beings. Here, the Creator's original form before the act of creation is seen as that of a serpent coiled round upon itself, implying that the creation of the world is a process of uncoiling—an unfolding into time and space.

Interestingly, the text we have chosen for Amun's reply seems to refer to the end of a cycle of creation. We have already seen how Ra-Atum generated everything from himself: this manifestation takes place in space, but it must also take place in time or there would be no time for anything to happen. This is why, in this text, the Creator says that he has passed millions of years between himself and the Inert One, that is Osiris. Osiris, as we have already seen, belongs to the third generation that emanates from Ra, but in truth he is a form of Ra himself. Osiris is of the last generation of gods before Horus who was believed to be incarnate in the pharaoh; and upon death, the pharaoh was believed to become Osiris, the god of death and resurrection. As we shall later see, Osiris may be regarded also as each and every human being who is on the spiritual path and knows his or her true nature as a being containing the divine spark. Osiris therefore represents the furthest point of creation in both space and time, the furthest point to which the Creator extends himself and divides himself into separate individuals before reversing the process: "mounds will be towns and towns will be mounds" and everything will eventually return to the Divine Source in "the one place." The "myriads of years" that Ra-Atum or Amen-Ra passes between himself and Osiris is the temporal equivalent of the "multitudes of things which came into being" when Ra-Atum generated the whole of creation out of himself. A single life-time is a tiny fraction of the Creator's uncoiling in time as a great serpent, just as an individual person is a tiny fraction of the Creator's spatial coming into being as Khepera.

THREE

PTAH

Invocation

Praisegiving to Ptah, lord of Maat,
King of the Two Lands,
Fair of face on his great seat,
The One God among the Ennead,
Beloved as King of the Two Lands.
May he give life, prosperity, health,
Alertness, favors and affection . . .

—*Votive Stela of Neferabu, from Deir el-Medina, in* Ancient Egyptian Literature, *Volume II, by Miriam Lichtheim, p. 109.*

Heart took shape in the form of Atum, Tongue took shape in the form of Atum. It is Ptah, the very great, who has given life to all the gods and their kas through this heart and through this tongue, from which Horus had come forth as Ptah, from which Thoth had come forth as Ptah.

Thus heart and tongue rule over all the limbs in accordance with the teaching that [he] is in everybody and [he] is in every mouth of all gods, all men, all cattle, all creeping things, whatever lives, thinking whatever [he] wishes and commanding whatever [he] wishes.

His ... Ennead is before him as teeth and lips. They are the semen and hands of Atum. For the Ennead of Atum came into being through his semen and his fingers. But the

Ennead is the teeth and lips in this mouth which pronounced the name of every thing, from which Shu and
Tefnut came forth, and which gave birth to the Ennead. . . .

> He gave birth to the gods,
> He made the towns,
> He established the nomes,
> He placed the gods in their shrines,
> He settled their offerings,
> He established their shrines,
> He made their bodies according to their wishes.
> Thus the gods entered into their bodies,
> Of every wood, every stone, every clay,
> Everything that grows upon him
> In which they came to be.
> Thus were gathered to him all the gods and their kas,
> Content, united with the Lord of the Two Lands.
>
> —*Shabaka Stone, in* Ancient Egyptian Literature, *Volume I, by
> Miriam Lichtheim, pp. 54–5.*

Reply

My likeness is created, and that is how this my name of Ptah
came into being; one fair of face, mighty of strength, to
whom men appeal within the castle of the Lord of Life . . .

> —Coffin Texts, *spell 647, translation by R. O. Faulkner, p. 75.*

Ptah is the creator god who was worshipped at Memphis
(the Greek name for Men-nefer). He is represented as a
mummiform man wearing a distinctive cap and carrying

a scepter. He is standing on a platform that symbolizes Maat. Ptah's consort is the lioness goddess Sekhmet. These two deities, together with their son Nefertum, were worshipped as a divine triad.

Ptah is the architect god and patron of craftsmen—as indicated in the second text used above for the invocation, where an emphasis is placed on his skill in making statues as bodies for the gods. The ancient Egyptians believed that the devotional statues in temples were vehicles through which the deities manifested, thus there was actually a divine presence within statues. As described in part one, chapter 4, a special ceremony called the Opening of the Mouth was performed to bring a statue to life in this way by awakening its senses. It would then be presented with food, drink, and other offerings. The same rite was performed on mummified bodies to bring the deceased to life in the afterlife. Ptah was said to have devised this ceremony. The belief that a deity can manifest through a wonder-working statue is condemned as idolatry in the monotheistic religions, yet it is still found today in Catholicism in the cult of the Virgin Mary, and in Hinduism, where the practice of making food offerings to divine statues is similar to that carried on in ancient Egypt and other ancient Pagan cultures.

In Memphite theology, a creation myth was devised that placed Ptah as the Supreme Being by subsuming other gods as aspects of Ptah or parts of his body. This myth has survived on the Shabaka Stone, named after a king of the Twenty-fifth Dynasty (c. 710 BC). It is a large basalt slab that, unfortunately, was partly damaged when it was used as a millstone, but it is now in the British Museum. Although the stone itself dates from the New Kingdom, the text inscribed on it may be considerably older, as it purports to be a work discovered in an old, damaged manuscript and copied onto the stone to preserve it. The second of the two texts in the invocation above is an extract from the inscription on this stone. According to the Memphite cosmogony, Ptah created the world by means of his heart and tongue, which took the form of Atum, the creator god of Heliopolis. The Heliopolitan Ennead, described in the text of the Shabaka Stone as the semen and hands or fingers of Atum, are also said to be the teeth and lips of Ptah. Horus and Thoth are here described as forms of Ptah and seem to be identified with his heart and tongue respectively. It is typical of Ptah to take on various divine identities, for he is syncretized with other gods as Ptah-ta-Tanen, Ptah-Nun, Ptah-Seker-Tem, Ptah-Asar, and others.

Ptah's method of creation is very much an intellectual approach: he conceives the idea in his heart and utters the creative word with his tongue, teeth, and lips. For the ancient Egyptians, the heart was the seat of consciousness, the basic self and conscience of a person. Nowadays we tend to regard the brain in this light, but the Egyptians seem to have had little idea of the function of the brain. During the process of mummification, the brain was removed and destroyed when it surely would have been preserved in the same way as other vital organs, such as the lungs and intestines, if its importance had been recognized. When Ptah relies on his heart for his creativity, this is not to be taken to mean that he becomes emotional, for his heart, as his essential self, is the organ of thinking and reasoning in a sincere, heartfelt way, and not the symbol of sentimental love and emotion that it has become today. The ancient Egyptians would not have made a distinction between rationality and emotionality in the way that we do: for them, reason, emotion, and personal integrity were all centered in the heart.

In the Memphite cosmogony, Ptah's tongue, which utters the creative word, is identified with Atum and Thoth, both creator gods in their own right, but here presented as aspects of Ptah. This myth shows the importance placed by the Egyptians on the idea of words of power and magical utterances. As explained in part one, chapter 7, words of power were very often the names of the deities, but not necessarily the names by which they were commonly known. The deities also had secret names; the secret names of the most important deities were the most powerful of all the words of power. The word or name had to be uttered with the correct pronunciation and intonation, however, to be effective. Magical texts that have survived from the late period of Egyptian civilization give instructions suggesting that magical words were chanted or intoned in a prolonged manner.

Ptah as the Creator bears strong similarities to the Judeo–Christian Creator. The second text of the invocation above makes it clear that he is both a transcendent (separate from the material world) deity and an immanent (within the material world) deity. As an immanent deity, he manifests through all living things in the same way as Khepera, the immanent manifestation of Ra-Atum, although in the case of Ptah, the mental faculties are emphasized; but Ptah also seems somewhat separate from his creation, rather intellectual and aloof, thoughtful and commanding; he is seen as an architectual designer, and sculptor making physical forms. It is a very different approach from that of Atum, who is so emotionally and physically involved in his creation; yet, ultimately, each god is an alternative way to conceive the one Creator.

FOUR

NEITH

Invocation

Father of the fathers and Mother of the mothers, the
divinity who came into being was in the midst of the
primeval waters having appeared out of herself
while the land was in twilight
and no land had yet come forth
and no plant had yet grown.
She illuminated the rays of her two eyes
and dawn came into being.
Then she said: let this place become land for me
in the midst of the primeval water
in order that I might rest on it.

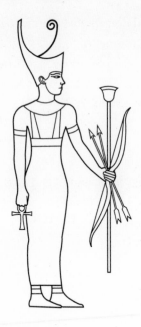

And this place became land in the midst of the primeval
   water, just as she said,
and thus came into being "the land of the waters"
   and Sais. . . .
Then she was pleased with this mound,
and thus Egypt came into being in jubilation.

—*Inscription in the Temple at Esna, translation by B. J. Kemp, in* Ancient Egypt: Anatomy of a Civilization, *pp. 37-43.*

You are the Lady of Sais . . .
   whose two-thirds are masculine
   and one-third is feminine
Unique Goddess, mysterious and great
who came to be in the beginning

and caused everything to come to be . . .
the divine mother of Ra, who shines in the horizon
the mysterious one who radiates her brightness.

> —Inscription in the Temple at Esna, translation by L. H. Lesko, in
> Religion in Ancient Egypt: Gods, Myths and Personal Practice,
> pp. 88-92.

Reply

I am all that has been, and is, and that shall be, and my robe
no mortal has yet uncovered.

> —Inscription in the Temple of Neith at Sais, according to Plutarch,
> translation by Frank Cole Babbitt, in Moralia, 354 c.

The impression given so far may be that the ancient Egyptians always conceived of the Creator as male, albeit with some female attributes. This is not so, for Neith (Nit, Net; pronounced "Neet"), a very important and ancient goddess whose main cult center was at Sais (Zau, now called Sa el-Hagar) in the western delta of Lower Egypt, was regarded as another form of the Creator. Although the second text above describes her as two-thirds masculine, this indicates her qualities rather than her gender. As explained in the chapter on Ra-Atum, when the Egyptians regarded the Supreme Being as male, they saw him as possessing also a female aspect, and here in the case of Neith we see that, although she is female, she is Father as well as Mother and possesses male qualities. She is represented as a woman wearing the red crown of Lower Egypt, and her symbol is a shield over two crossed arrows. Barbara S. Lesko points out that the "shield" was originally two click beetles facing one another with their heads together (1999, p. 46).

Neith is associated with the crown—the power of the king and political power; hunting; and prowess in battle. The Greek's placed emphasis on her warlike qualities and associated her with Athena. She is also a protector of the dead and is one of the four guardian goddesses (along with Isis, Nephthys, and Serket) whose image was found protecting the shrine of Tutankhamun. Like Hathor, she welcomes the dead into the afterlife. She became associated with mummy wrappings, as she was regarded as the inventor of weaving, and sometimes her click beetle symbol has been misinterpreted as a weaver's shuttle. Her patronage of weaving also symbolically indicates her power over fate or destiny, which seems to be alluded to in the famous inscription (said to have been) in her temple, and quoted in her reply above.

This connection with weaving, traditionaly a female activity, shows that it would be a mistake to think of her as having a masculine personality, for she presides over women's concerns as well as the traditionaly male pursuits of politics and warfare. As a sky goddess and mother of Ra, she takes the form of a cow, like Nut and Hathor. In this form she is called Ihet and bears the epithet "the Great Cow." Her roles as virgin mother and Creatrix are often overlooked but remain important features to emphasize (Lesko, 1999).

Neith's consort at Esna is the ram god Khnum, but in the Pyramid Age (third millennium BC), she was linked with Set and seen as the mother of Sobek, the crocodile god sometimes regarded as a form of Set. Occasionally, Neith herself was portrayed with the head of a crocodile and was regarded as "mother of crocodiles." She is also the mother of the chaos serpent Apep, who is said to have come into being from her spittle. Her relationship with Set, however, was not always recognized. In *The Contendings of Horus and Set* (an ancient document not published separately, but which appears in translation in Kaster, 1995), she takes the side of Horus against Set in their struggle for the throne. She recommends that Set be compensated for yielding the throne to Horus by providing him with two Syrian goddesses, Astarte and Anat, as wives. This may be a reference to her role as protector of the institution of marriage and scarcely indicates that she is herself Set's wife.

The first text in the invocation above is from an inscription in the Temple of Khnum at Esna. Here we see that, like Ra-Atum, Neith produces a mound of earth out of the primeval waters; and, like his, her eyes generate light. Neith's manner of creation, however, is like that of Ptah, uttering a word of command. Both Ptah and Neith have similarities with the Judeo–Christian Creator in this respect and also in their being pleased with their work of creation, which is mentioned in their myths. Neith also has something in common with the creator god Khnum with whom she was linked at Esna, for like him, she was associated with the annual Nile flood and the return of life after the waters receded.

Once again it is apparent that the different Egyptian cosmogonies do not directly contradict one another but are variations on the same theme. Also, the various creator deities are not so much distinct entities as the same single

Creator viewed in slightly different ways and with different emphases. In Neith, we see the Supreme Being as Mother. It is interesting to note, however, that this form of the Deity, known for bringing about the beneficent aspects of creation, also produces the evil entity Apep and is associated with the destructive gods Set and Sobek. As we have already seen, the Egyptians never ignored the darker side of life, needing to account for evil and suffering by some act of the gods in the First Time, which introduced a destructive principle in creation—usually identified as Apep, Nak, or Set.

It has to be said that Neith seems not to have inspired the same level of following among modern devotees of Egyptian deities as have some other goddesses, particularly Hathor, Isis, Nut, and Sekhmet. This may be partly due to a lack of primary source material about her—she appears little in the *Pyramid Texts*, the inscription at Esna being the only account of her creation myth, and no other myths about her survive—but is probably largely due to the fact that these other important goddesses have assumed Neith's role. Yet for the ancient Egyptians themselves, Neith was a very important goddess. Although Hathor, Nut, and Isis rival her as mother goddesses; Sekhmet performs her fierce protective and destructive functions; and despite Isis being acknowledged as the Creatrix by the time the Greeks ruled Egypt, Neith is the only Egyptian goddess recognized as the Supreme Being on a par with the male gods, and it may be that she was recognized as such from the earliest era. She may have even been regarded as the national goddess of Lower Egypt, and her presence at Esna could have been an attempt to claim her for Upper Egypt as well.

FIVE

KHNUM

Invocation

    Another hymn to Khnum-Ra,
    God of the potter's wheel,
    Who settled the land by his handiwork;
    Who joins in secret,
    Who builds soundly,
    Who nourishes the nestlings
      by the breath of his mouth;
    Who drenches the land with Nun,
    While round sea and great ocean surround him.

He has fashioned gods and men,
He has formed flocks and herds;
He made birds as well as fishes,
He created bulls, engendered cows. . . .

Formed all on his potter's wheel,
Their speech differs in each region,
And clashes with that of Egypt.
He created precious things in their lands,
That they might bear their products abroad,
For the lord of the wheel is their father too,
Tatenen who made all that is on their soil. . . .

All your creatures give you thanks,
You are Ptah-Tatenen, creator of creators,
Who in Iunyt brought forth all that is. . . .

He made plants in the field,
He dotted the shores with flowers;
He made fruit trees bear their fruit,
To fill the needs of men and gods.
He opened seams in the bellies of mountains,
He made the quarries spew out their stones.

... Beneficent god,
Contenting god,
God who forms bodies,
God who equips nostrils,
God who binds the Two Lands,
So that they join their natures.

When Nun and Tatenen first came into being,
They appeared as lotus on his back,
As heir to Djed-shepsy at the start.
Their ka will not perish,
None shall hinder their action,
No land is lacking all that he made.
They are concealed among mankind,
Creating all beings since god's time,
They are alive and abiding,
Like Ra rising and setting ...

—*The Great Hymn of Praise to Khnum, from the Temple of Esna, in*
Ancient Egyptian Literature, *Volume III, by Miriam Lichtheim,*
pp. 112–15.

Reply

I am Khnemu the Creator. My hands rest upon thee to protect thy person, and to make sound thy body. I gave thee thine heart. . . . I am he who created himself. I am the primeval watery abyss, and I am Nile who riseth at his will to give health for me to those who toil. I am the guide and director of all men, the Almighty, the father of the gods, Shu, the mighty possessor of the earth.

> —Inscription of King Tcheser on a rock on the Island of Sahal,
> translation by E. A. Wallis Budge, in The Gods of the Egyptians,
> Volume II, pp. 53–4.

Khnum (pronounced "Kanoom"), or Khnemu, is the creator god who was worshipped in the form of a ram or ram-headed man on the island of Elephantine (at modern Aswan, called Swenet by the ancient Egyptians) and Esna (Iunyt). At Elephantine, where he may have been worshipped from the Early Dynastic Period (3100–2686 BC), he was guardian of the Nile's source, controller of the annual inundation, and formed a triad with two goddesses: his wife Satet (Satis to the Greeks) and their daughter Anuket (Anqet or Anukis, sometimes regarded as a daughter of Ra). At Esna, he was the potter god who created the physical forms of everything, and also created the ka (the so-called double) of every person. This role as divine potter is very much apparent in the hymn used for the invocation above.

The ancient Egyptian word for "ram" is the onomatopoeic *ba*, but the term for "soul" is also *ba*, so the Egyptians were able to make a pun on this when they called Khnum the Ba of

Ra. At night, when the ba (soul) of Ra is in the underworld, it may be depicted as Khnum with the head of a ba (ram). In this way, Khnum could be identified with Ra as Khnum-Ra, as in the invocation above. This hymn also refers to him as Khnum-Ptah. Khnum has much in common with Ptah, the Creator and craftsman god who makes physical forms. Tatenen, also mentioned in the hymn, is the earth god of the primeval mound who, as we have seen in the chapter on Ptah, was syncretized with Ptah as Ptah-ta-Tanen.

It is interesting that one stanza of the hymn that we have used for the invocation mentions that Khnum is the father of foreign people and Creator of things in countries outside Egypt. Although it may seem obvious that a creator god creates everything, not just one country, it is surprising how frequently one comes across the idea that Pagan deities are firmly restricted to the land in which they were first worshipped and that it is strange or even wrong to be following an Egyptian form of Paganism if one is living in a country other than Egypt. Contrary to a common misconception that people of ancient times were insular, untraveled, and ignorant of other countries, there was certainly knowledge of other peoples, other places, and other cultures, even though most people did not travel abroad in the way that they do now. This same stanza, referring to Khnum as the father of foreigners, demonstrates that the ancient Egyptians had the concept of a universal Deity, and that they would not, in principle, have regarded it as inappropriate for Egyptian deities to be worshipped in foreign countries.

The *Westcar Papyrus* features Khnum in a story called "King Cheops and the Magicians," which is about the birth of three princes who were destined to become the first kings of the Fifth Dynasty. Khnum was one of many deities to attend the birth. It is said, he put health into the children's bodies. This may imply that he breathed life into them, which correlates with the claim in the first stanza of the hymn above that he nourishes nestlings with his breath. At Esna, Khnum was venerated as a manifestation of the air god Shu, as in the god's reply above. Elsewhere he was regarded as the *ba* (manifestation) of Geb, the earth god, and of Osiris, the god of death and resurrection.

Because of his association with the Nile flood, Khnum was known as "lord of crocodiles," which also links him with his consort at Esna, Neith, who, as we have already seen, was called "mother of crocodiles" and is the mother of the crocodile god Sobek.

SIX

THOTH

Invocation

Come to me, Thoth, O noble Ibis,
O god who loves Khmun;
O letter-writer of the Ennead,
Great one who dwells in Un!
Come to me and give me counsel,
Make me skillful in your calling;
Better is your calling than all callings,
It makes men great.
He who masters it is found fit to hold office . . .
You are he who offers counsel,

Fate and Fortune are with you,
Come to me and give me counsel,
I am a servant of your house,
Let me tell of your valiant deeds,
Wheresoever I may be;
Then the multitudes will say:
"Great are they, the deeds of Thoth!"

—*Papyrus Anastasi V, in* Ancient Egyptian Literature, *Volume II, by Miriam Lichtheim, p. 113.*

Reply

I am Thoth, the perfect scribe, whose hands are pure, the lord of the two horns, who maketh iniquity to be destroyed, the scribe of right and truth, who abominateth sin. Behold, he is the writing-reed of the god Neb-er-tcher, the lord of laws, who giveth forth the speech of wisdom and under-standing, whose words have dominion over the two lands. I am Thoth, the lord of right and truth, who trieth the right and the truth for the gods, the judge of words in their essence, whose words triumph over violence. I have scattered the darkness, I have driven away the whirlwind and the storm, and I have given the pleasant breeze of the north wind unto Osiris Un-nefer as he came forth from the womb of her who gave him birth. I have made Ra to set as Osiris, and Osiris setteth as Ra setteth. I have made him to enter into the hidden habitation to vivify the heart of the Still-Heart, the holy soul, who dwelleth in Amentet, and to shout cries of joy unto the Still-Heart, Un-nefer, the son of Nut.

I am Thoth, the favored one of Ra, the lord of might, who bringeth to a prosperous end that which he doeth, the mighty one of enchantments who is in the boat of millions of years, the lord of laws, the subduer of the two lands, whose words of might gave strength to her that gave him birth, whose word doeth away with opposition and fight-ing, and who performeth the will of Ra in his shrine.

—Book of the Dead, *chapter 182, translation by E. A. Wallis Budge.*

Closing

Oh my twice-great master Thoth,
The Only One,
Who has no equal,
Who sees and hears whoever passes.

Who knows whoever comes,
With the knowledge of everything that happens!
You have made my heart walk upon your waters,
He who walks on your road will never stumble.

—*Petosiris, in* The Living Wisdom of Ancient Egypt, *by Christian
Jacq, p. 42.*

Thoth is the Greek rendering of the Egyptian name Dje-
huty or Tahuti. Thoth was also identified by the Greeks
with their god Hermes and was called Hermes Trismegistus
to distinguish him from the Greek form of Hermes. The
title Trismegistus, meaning "three times great," is a Greek
translation of the Egyptian expression, *pa aa, pa aa, pa aa,*
meaning "the great, the great, the great," which was often
applied to Thoth. He was also sometimes called "twice-
great," as in the closing prayer above. There are even texts
that describe him as "eight times great" or "nine times great."
The main cult center of Thoth was Hermopolis, which is
now called el-Ashmunein. His totem animals are the baboon
and the ibis and he is often represented as a man with the
head of an ibis.

One of the most important deities of ancient Egypt, he
was credited with being a creator god; the closing prayer
above shows that he is indeed the Only One, the Supreme
Being; specifically, in this case, the Divine Mind or intelli-
gence of God, the Logos or Word of God (the ordering principle of the universe). E. A. Wallis Budge (1969 [1904], Vol.
II, pp. 516–17) points to parallels between the Memphite,
Hermopolitan, and Heliopolitan cosmogonies whereby

Thoth, as the mental aspect of Ptah (manifesting through Ptah's tongue, as we explained in the chapter on Ptah), can be seen as a form of Shu, who is the first emanation of Atum. This has led to Thoth's and Shu's respective consorts, Maat and Tefnut, also being identified with one another, and furthermore, to Ptah's consort, Sekhmet, becoming identified with Maat and Tefnut.

Thoth is the god of wisdom, "lord of the divine words," and patron of scribes and physicians. These qualities are very apparent from the texts selected above, particularly the invocation in which his "calling" refers to the profession of scribes who were much valued in ancient Egypt. It is Thoth who is said to have devised hieroglyphic writing, but his role as lord of the divine words probably means more than this: It was Thoth who prescribed the correct practices and appropriate forms of ritual to be carried out in all the temples and the sacred texts used there were written by him. In discussing the importance of Thoth's writing, Patrick Boylan (1999, p. 95) quotes from a hymn that describes Thoth as "he who has given words and script, who makes the temples to prosper, who founds shrines, and who makes the gods to know what is needful (i.e., sacrifice and ritual)."

Thoth is one of several deities to whom special magical powers are attributed; the source of his magic is his great knowledge and his command of words—how to use and pronounce words with magical effectiveness. His medical knowledge is closely connected to his magical abilities. Magic was regarded by the Egyptians as an important aspect of medical treatment. Often, the reciting of a spell was required as the medicine was taken. In the texts that we have used above, Thoth's purity and his reliance on right and truth are also stressed, ensuring that his formidable powers are only employed for just purposes.

Thoth is a moon god. It is notable that the Egyptians had lunar gods and solar goddesses, whereas many other cultures strictly see the sun as male and the moon as female. The Egyptians also had an earth god (Geb) and a sky goddess (Nut), which again is the reverse of what is found in other cultures. One of the myths about Thoth says that when Nut was pregnant, Ra forbade her to give birth on any day of the year, so Thoth played a game of checkers with the moon, Aah, and won enough of the moon's light to create five extra days in which Nut's five children could be born. This is a symbolic way of describing the fact that the lunar year, consisting of twelve months of thirty days each (the time from each new moon to the next), has 360 days, whereas the solar year (summer solstice to summer solstice, or winter solstice to winter solstice) has 365 days. Ancient agricultural societies kept track of the passage of time by noticing the phases of the moon (the first calendars being lunar) so the moon became associated with the measurement of time, and then with measurement in general—such as the measurement of lengths, distances, and quantities. Thoth's rational faculty and his discernment in judgment may derive from his abilities as a moon god to count and measure accurately.

Thoth was regarded as Ra's night deputy, and was also one of the occupants in Ra's solar bark. The reference to Ra setting as Osiris, in Thoth's reply above, means that the setting of the sun was regarded as the death of Ra, who then became identified with Osiris as the god of the dead. (We shall return to this point in the chapter on Osiris.) Thoth, as lord of time and the divine order of the universe, could be seen as being in charge of this process of death and renewal.

When Osiris was a king of Egypt in mythical times, Thoth was his vizier. He was the protector of Isis after Osiris was murdered by Set, teaching Isis the skills of magic, and helping her to protect Horus, the son she had by Osiris, against the machinations of Set. When Horus was old enough to challenge the usurper Set for the throne, Thoth was his advocate, using his considerable skills of articulate persuasion to plead Horus's cause at the tribunal of the gods. Thoth also defended Osiris against false accusations made by Set, clearing the murdered god's reputation and declaring him "true of voice," which enabled Osiris to assume his role as lord and judge of the dead.

An alternative strand of myth, which presents Thoth as the brother of Set and in league with him against Osiris, is generally played down (*Pyramid Texts*, utterances 218–19). Thoth is also, perhaps surprisingly, regarded as the son of Set and Horus, and more often, as the son of Ra. (This will be explained in the chapter on Set.) The association with Set does not in any way reflect badly on Thoth's character, for in myths where the other deities are sometimes shown in a bad light, his conduct is consistently impeccable.

Other myths about Thoth show him to be the god who restores the Eye, whether it be the solar Eye of Ra or the lunar Eye of Horus. When Ra's angry Eye took the form of a lioness and went raging off, abandoning Egypt, who better than Thoth to entice her back again with his soothing words and skill of eloquence. In this context, Patrick Boylan cites Thoth's epithets: "soother of the gods," "cool of mouth," and "sweet of tongue" (1999, p. 128). Thoth also restores Horus's Eye—often called the Wedjat Eye, meaning "whole eye" or "sound eye"—after it has been injured by Set during their long conflict. This Wedjat Eye represents the moon, which becomes small during its waning, as if consumed by the malign influence of Set, as god of darkness, but then grows larger and becomes whole again under the healing influence of Thoth. (This will be addressed in more detail in later chapters on Set and Horus.)

In the text chosen for the reply, Thoth is "lord of the two horns," perhaps in the sense that the crescent moon may be said to be horned. Also, like other Egyptian gods, he was sometimes referred to as a bull. The terms "son of Nut" and "Still-Heart" refer to Osiris. As god of justice, reason, and balance, Thoth has an important role in the judgment hall of Osiris—where the heart of the deceased is weighed in the scales of Maat to see if he or she is of sufficient moral integrity to be allowed into the blessed afterlife, to live with the gods. He helps Anubis weigh the hearts and carefully records the verdict on his scroll. The text also shows that Thoth "doeth away with opposition and fighting" in that he resolved the dispute between Horus and Set. He claims to have "driven away the whirlwind and the storm," which are phenomena very much associated with Set, the god of chaos. In the reply above we also find Maat to be the wife of Thoth. Another wife of his is the goddess Sesheta or Seshat, who is a scribe and librarian, sometimes identified with Nephthys.

All scientific learning and sacred wisdom was attributed to Thoth, so in principle he was regarded as the author of the great books of knowledge, medicine, sacred texts, and spells that were collected in the temples and handed down for generations. In much later times, the Greek *Hermetica* were attributed to him under his name of Hermes Trismegistus (appear in translation by Scott, 1993).

SEVEN

HATHOR

Invocation

Hathor, Lady of Amentet, mighty dweller in the funeral mountain, lady of Ta-tchesert, daughter . . . of Ra, dweller before him, beautiful of face in the Boat of millions of years, the habitation . . . of peace, creator of law in the boat of the favored ones . . .

—Book of the Dead, *chapter 186, translation by E. A. Wallis Budge.*

O you lords of the western sky,
O you gods of the western sky,
O you who rule the shores of the western sky,
Who rejoice at Hathor's coming,

Who love to see her beauty rise!
I let her know, I say at her side
That I rejoice in seeing her!
My hands do "come to me, come to me,"
My body says, my lips repeat:
Holy music for Hathor, music a million times,
Because you love music, million times music
To your ka wherever you are!
I am he who makes the singer waken music for Hathor,
Every day at any hour she wishes.
May your heart be at peace with music,
May you proceed in goodly peace,

May you rejoice in life and gladness
With Horus who loves you,
Who feasts with you on your foods,
Who eats with you of the offerings,
May you admit me to it every day!

—*Stela of King Wahankh Intef II, in* Ancient Egyptian Literature,
Volume I, by Miriam Lichtheim, p. 95.

Reply

I am Hathor who brings her Horus and who proclaims her
Horus; and my heart is the lion-god . . . there is no limit to
my vision, there are none who can encircle my arms, every
god will take himself off before me. I have appeared as
Hathor, the Primeval, the Lady of All, who lives on truth; I
am the uraeus who lives on truth, who lifts up the faces of
all the gods, and all the gods are beneath my feet. I am She
who displays his beauty and assembles his powers, I am
that Eye of Horus, the female messenger of the Sole Lord,
the like of whom shall not be again. Truly I am She who
made his name. I have flourished, I came into being before
the sky was fashioned, and it gives me praise; before the
earth was released and it exalts me, while I seek your saliva
and your spittle; they are Shu and Tefnut. I have searched
and sought out, and see, I have fetched what I sought; come
with my horns and display my beauty; come with my face
and I will cause you to be exalted. I have smitten all with
my hands in this my name of Hathor; I have given my
tears. I reduce them to order in this my name of She who is
over reducing to order; I make warmth for them in this my

name of Shesmetet. Such am I; I am Edjo, I am indeed the Mistress of the Two Lands.

—Coffin Texts, *spell 331, translation by R. O. Faulkner.*

Hathor (Het-heru, Het-heret) is one of the major goddesses, and her main cult center was at Dendera (Iunet) in Upper Egypt. She is represented in human form or as a cow, and has been identified with a cow goddess worshipped in Egypt from the earliest times. The cow is an important goddess image, symbolizing the gentle, nurturing qualities of a mother. Hathor is one of the goddesses regarded as the Eye of Ra, which, as we have seen, is both an aspect of the Creator and the feminine principle within the Supreme Being. The areas of life that she presides over are love, beauty, cosmetics, sexuality, music, and dance; she is in particular the goddess of women; she also welcomes the dead into the afterlife, which was associated with the western horizon (where the sun goes down). As the Eye of Ra, she is essentially a solar goddess and her qualities are expressive of the beneficent, life-giving powers of the sun.

The first of the texts we have chosen for the invocation above shows her to be the daughter of Ra and one of the occupants in the solar bark of millions of years. As the creator of law, Hathor is identified here with Maat as the essential feminine principle. Amentet is the realm of the dead and Ta-tchesert is the sacred land.

The second text shows her association with music and dance and also mentions her relationship with Horus. Hathor's name means "House of Horus," the term "house" here being the word used for a temple rather than a domestic home. "House" may also be used metaphorically to mean "womb," for Hathor was originally the mother of the younger form of Horus before Isis came to be seen as his mother (Lesko, 1999, p. 82). As a sky goddess, Hathor is also a "house" in the sense of being the abode of Horus as the sun. The elder form of Horus, worshipped at Edfu, is the husband of Hathor. An important festival called the Feast of the Joyous Union, celebrating their marriage, used to take place in early summer, about the time of May to June.

In Hathor's reply above, although she calls herself the Eye of Horus, which is often a symbol of the moon, she is clearly here identifying Horus with Ra. She is referring to the Heliopolitan creation myth that we have already examined, in which the Eye went in search of the lost Shu and Tefnut (the two deities formed from Ra-Atum's spittle). When she says "I have given my tears," she is referring to the myth of Ra's Eye creating humans from tears. At the same time, parts of this passage could be translated as Ra's own voice. If the word translated as "with" is rendered instead as "on," the following passage may be spoken by Ra: "come with my horns and display my beauty; come with my face and I will cause you to be exalted." The phrase could then be seen as referring to his attempt to placate the goddess by placing her as a cobra on the front of his crown (horns) or brow. Hathor even identifies herself here with Edjo or Wadjet, the cobra goddess who is the tutelary deity of Upper Egypt, represented as the uraeus symbol on the pharaoh's crown.

Hathor also says of her tears that she "reduced them to order." This refers to another myth about Hathor, which appears in the *Book of the Divine Cow*, in which Ra sent her to punish human beings because they were in rebellion against divine authority by speaking blasphemously against him (Kaster, 1995 includes a translation of this story). Hathor changed to her fierce form, the lioness goddess Sekhmet, and went berserk, killing everyone she could find. She would not come back when Ra repented of his decision to punish humans and could be pacified only when he arranged for gallons of beer to be poured out to make her drunk. It is tempting to think that this story may have originated in the account of a meteor coming close to the earth, a phenomenon that has occasionally been witnessed in modern times. A meteor is an enormous ball of fire with a flaming tail, filling the sky with a holocaust of fire as it roars along, burning up in the atmosphere.

There is another myth about the Eye leaving Egypt and refusing to return. She is eventually brought back by Onuris (Anher), "he who brought back the Distant One." He is a hunter god worshipped at Thinnis. In another version of the story, it is the goddess Tefnut as the Eye in the form of a lioness who goes south into Nubia. Thoth and Shu are sent by Ra to look for her and she is pacified and brought back by Thoth, who gently cajoles her into accompanying Shu and himself home. As she calms down on the way back, she turns into a cat (possibly Bast, the cat goddess) and finally bathes in the Nile on her return to Egypt, where she reverts to her original form as a woman. This myth would seem to signify something rather different from the first story of the errant Eye—probably the phenomenon of the sun moving southward in the sky as the winter draws on and the climate becomes cooler. Egyptian winters can occasionally be surprisingly harsh with rainstorms and flash flooding (Lesko, 1999, p. 145). At the winter solstice, the sun reaches its farthest position south and begins to return.

In other contexts, Hathor is seen as a gentle and kindly goddess. In the papyrus called *The Contendings of Horus and Set* (c. 1150 BC, trans. in Kaster, 1995), she cheers up her father Ra by exposing herself erotically to him when he is in a bad mood after having been insulted by one of the other gods, and restores Horus's vision after he has been blinded by Set. The former episode is indicative of an older role for Hathor, in which she was Ra's consort rather than his daughter.

One of Hathor's symbols is a sacred sycamore tree, which, like the cow, represents her qualities of fertility and nurturing, especially in the afterlife, in which context she is sometimes depicted emerging from a tree to provide sustenance for the dead. Her sacred instrument is the sistrum (a kind of rattle), often decorated on both sides with a cow-eared woman's face representing Hathor herself, or Bat, a cow goddess assimilated to her. The menat, a necklace of large beads probably used as another sort of rattle, is also sacred to Hathor.

EIGHT

SEKHMET AND BAST

Invocation

Homage to thee, O Sekhmet-Bast-Ra, thou mistress of the
gods, thou bearer of wings, lady of the Anes bandlet, queen
of the crowns of the South and of the North, only One,
sovereign of her father, superior to whom the gods cannot
be, thou mighty one of enchantments in the Boat of Millions of Years, thou who art pre-eminent, who risest in the
seat of silence . . . mistress and lady of the tomb, mother in
the horizon of heaven, gracious one, beloved, destroyer of
rebellion, offerings are in thy grasp, and thou art standing in
the bows of the boat of thy divine father to overthrow the

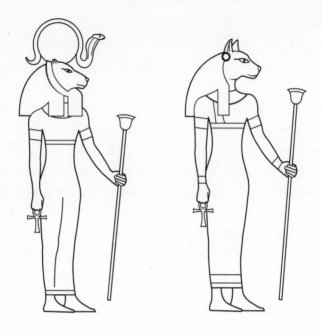

Fiend. Thou hast placed Maat in the bows of his boat. . . . Praise be to thee, O lady, who art mightier than the gods, and words of adoration rise to thee from the Eight gods. The living souls who are in their chests praise thy mystery. O thou who art their mother, thou source from whom they sprang, who makest for them a place of repose in the hidden underworld, who makest sound their bones and preservest them from terror, who makest them strong in the abode of everlastingness, who preservest them from the evil chamber of the souls of the god-of-the-terrible-face who is among the company of the gods. . . . "Utchat of Sekhmet, mighty lady, mistress of the gods" is thy name.

—Book of the Dead, *chapter 164, translation by E. A. Wallis Budge.*

Reply

I am the fiery Eye of Horus, which went forth terrible, Lady of Slaughter, greatly awesome, who came into being in the flame of the sunshine, to whom Ra granted appearings in glory, whose children Ra-Atum made enduring. What Ra said about her: Mighty is the fear of you, great is the awe of you, mighty is your striking-power, great is your magic in the bodies of your foes, and the hostile ones have fallen on their faces because of you; all men have been in the sleep of death because of you and through your power, and those who shall see you shall be afraid of you in this vigorous form of yours which the Lord of the Enneads has given to you—so he spoke of me, so said the Lord of the Enneads of me. I have become the Eye of Horus . . . I am indeed she who shoots . . . I am she who triumphs, the companion of Ra.

Behold me, men and gods! Set the face of me and create awe of me on that plateau of the Stone of Brightness. Behold me, men and gods! I have come into being as the Lady of Glorious Appearings, I have reappeared in glory, I have made my being enduring, my flame is behind me, the awe of me is before me, I have conquered the gods, and there is no-one who can come opposing me—so say those who are in front of the Great Throne.

—Coffin Texts, *spell 316, translation by R. O. Faulkner.*

Sekhmet, another form of the sun goddess, is, like Hathor, one of the goddesses called the Eye of Ra. (In the text used for her reply above, the Eye is identified with the Eye of Horus.) She may be regarded as the fierce, destructive form of Hathor or of Mut. Bast, also called Bastet, may be regarded as a benign form of Sekhmet, but has lunar as well as solar associations.

Sekhmet is represented as a woman with the head of a lioness wearing a crown consisting of a solar disc with a uraeus. She is the consort of the creator god, Ptah, worshipped at Memphis (Men-nefer) and the mother of his son, Nefertum. The texts quoted above amply demonstrate her power and fierceness, showing how she was both admired and feared by the ancient Egyptians. In the text used for the invocation, she is Sekhmet-Bast-Ra, a form of Mut, a goddess often represented as a woman wearing a vulture headdress, although she also appears with the head of a lioness. This chapter in the *Book of the Dead*, however, is illustrated with a different image—that of a woman with three heads, winged arms, and a phallus. This would seem to represent the different forms of Mut, as vulture, woman, and lioness, combined with the masculine energy of Ra.

More than seven hundred large statues of Sekhmet were found at Mut's temple at Karnak. It has been speculated that this enormous number of statues was erected to placate the fiery goddess during a national crisis, when it may have seemed that Egypt was under attack from her (Lesko, 1999, p. 140). Sekhmet is called the Lady of Plague. It was believed that she was attended by a train of demonic powers that were responsible for sickness and disease, especially the outbreaks of plague that tended to afflict the country at about the time of the new year. The physical cause was an annual change in the climatic conditions that were conducive to an outbreak of plague, but the ancient Egyptians, despite the sophistication of their medical knowledge in some respects, did not understand this. The only means of protection to which they could resort were the amulets of Sekhmet, which they exchanged as New Year gifts, and magical spells and prayers appealing to the goddess for mercy.

That Sekhmet was regarded as a goddess of healing as well as destruction reveals an interesting principle in Egyptian thinking. A god or goddess believed to have caused disease or misfortune was also seen, quite logically, as having the power to withdraw those harmful influences. This view was also taken of Serket, the goddess who presides over scorpions and is therefore ultimately responsible if they sting anyone. However, it was also to Serket that people appealed for protection from scorpions and healing from their stings. Perhaps because of her power over these dangerous creatures she was also regarded as a protectress of the dead. A similar view was taken of Set, whose dangerous powers could also be drawn on for strength in battle and protection against the chaos serpent Apep, until in later times when Set himself became increasingly demonized and identified with Apep.

Despite Sekhmet's formidable destructive powers, her role as a bringer of plague, and the myth about her being sent by her father, Ra, to exterminate human beings, she was never demonized like Set. Both invocations above refer to her role in the bark of Ra, where she wards off the fiend, Apep. She protects the dead from demonic forces and provides her sunlight for the living. The first invocation links her with Maat, the divine feminine principle of order. As mentioned in the chapter on Thoth, Thoth can be seen as the mental aspect of Ptah, so Thoth's wife, Maat, can be identified with Ptah's wife, Sekhmet. This would seem to teach us that order and justice (Maat) can be maintained only by balancing gentle, benign, and merciful forces (Bast or the benevolent form of Sekhmet) against powerful, destructive, and punitive forces (Sekhmet in her vengeful aspect). Too much gentleness and indulgence would result in weakness and vulnerability to the forces of chaos, but too much strength and discipline would be stifling and destructive. This is why, in Egyptian theology, the Divine Feminine, represented by the Eye of Ra, has these two complementary aspects: the nurturing, loving aspect embodied in Hathor, and the destructive, vengeful aspect embodied in Sekhmet. The goddesses Mut, Bast, and Tefnut, also identified with the Eye of Ra, represent both aspects within themselves, but in less extreme form.

Sekhmet's priesthood specialized in healing, partly because, as the bringer of plague, she was regarded as being able to restrain the forces of disease that she controlled, but also because her strength was needed to fight off demons and evil spirits believed to be responsible for much disease. Ancient Egyptian medical papyri that have survived and have been used by priests of Sekhmet and doctors, show that the Egyptians took great care in diagnosing and treating a wide range of medical conditions and that they used herbal remedies, magical spells, and other kinds of treatment for them. However, the concept of infection was not understood, and even if it had been, the means of treating it would not necessarily have been available.

The cause of disease was attributed to the malign spells of enemies or the vengeance of an angry deity or spirit of a dead person whom one had perhaps offended in some way. The medical papyri reveal that often a doctor or priest could do little to help his patient except try to relieve pain and discomfort. It seems shocking and tragic that the people who had the knowledge and technical and artistic skills to build mighty temples and pyramids, which still astound us today, should be so vulnerable and helpless in the face of disease. Some of the treatments would seem to have done more harm than good: a combination of hot climate, infection, and a dusty environment made the Egyptians susceptible to eye ailments, but remedies involving an eye paint made of powdered stone would seem to have exacerbated the problem (Nunn, 1997, pp. 147 and 201). When blindness occurred, it was commonly attributed to the sufferer having provoked the wrath of some deity. For most of human history, the situation has been no better; it is only because of medical research over the past hundred years, the development of inoculations, antibiotics, cancer therapies, and advanced surgical techniques, that we are not in the same perilous condition today. A goddess such as Sekhmet is a reflection of the ancient Egyptians' sense that the universe is an awesome and dangerous place, ruled by unpredictable powers beyond human control, so it was as well to keep on the good side of such powers, treat them with reverence and avoid arousing their displeasure in the hope that they might be called on for help when a strong ally was needed. Nowadays, when we usually look for a scientific explanation for disease, we are less likely to see it as a sign of divine retribution. For this reason, modern followers of Sekhmet are unlikely to regard her as the bringer of disease, and tend to see her as primarily a healer and a powerful protector of all those who turn to her for help.

The invocation above could also be used to invoke Bast. She is usually portrayed as a woman with a cat's head, but sometimes has a lioness head instead; her symbols are the sistrum and the basket. Her cult center was at Bubastis (Per-Bastet) in Lower Egypt. She is associated with domesticity, pleasure, fertility, and healing. She also has nurturing, motherly qualities.

NINE

SHU

Invocation

Homage to thee, O flesh and bone of Ra, thou first-born son who didst proceed from his members, who wast chosen to be the chief of those who were brought forth, thou mighty one, thou divine form, who art endowed with strength as the lord of transformations. Thou overthrowest the Seba fiends each day. The divine boat hath the wind behind it, thy heart is glad. Those who are in the Antti boat utter loud cries of joy when they see Shu, the son of Ra, triumphant, and driving his spear into the serpent fiend Nekau. Ra setteth out to sail over the heavens at dawn daily. The goddess Tefnut is seated on thy head, she hurleth her

flames of fire against thy enemies, and maketh them to be destroyed utterly. Thou art equipped by Ra, thou art mighty through his words of power, thou art the heir of thy father upon his throne, and thy Doubles rest in the Doubles of Ra, even as the taste of what hath been in the mouth remaineth therein. . . . Homage to thee, O son of Ra, who wast begotten by Temu himself. Thou didst create thyself, and thou hadst no mother. Thou art truth, the lord of Truth, thou art the Power, the ruling power of the gods. Thou dost conduct the Eye of thy father Ra. They give gifts unto thee into thine own hands. Thou makest to be at peace the Great Goddess, when storms are passing over her. Thou dost stretch out the heavens on high, and dost establish them with thine own hands. Every god boweth in homage before thee, the

King of the South, the King of the North, Shu, the son of Ra, life strength and health be to thee! Thou, O great god Pautti, art furnished with the brilliance of the Eye of Ra in Heliopolis, to overthrow the Seba fiends on behalf of thy father. Thou makest the divine Boat to sail onwards in peace. The mariners who are therein exult, and all the gods shout for joy when they hear thy divine name. Greater, yea greater art thou than the gods in thy name of Shu, son of Ra.

—*Magical Harris Papyrus, number 501, translation by E. A. Wallis Budge, in* An Introduction to Ancient Egyptian Literature, *pp. 222–3.*

Reply

I am the soul of Shu at the head of the celestial kine, who ascends to heaven at his desire, who descends to earth at his wish. Come joyfully at meeting the god in me, for I am Shu whom Atum fashioned, and this garment of mine is the air of life. A cry for me went forth from the mouth of Atum, the air opened up upon my ways. It is I who make the sky light after darkness, my pleasant color is due to the air which goes forth after me from the mouth of Atum, and the storm-cloud of the sky is my efflux; hail-storms and half-darkness are my sweat. The length of this sky belongs to my strides, the width of this earth belongs to my settlements. I am he whom Atum created, and I am bound for my place of eternity. I am Everlasting, who fashioned the Chaos-gods, reproduced by the spittle of Atum which issued from his mouth when he used his hand; his saliva will be made to fall to the earth.

Thus said Atum: Tefnut is my living daughter, and she shall be with her brother Shu; "Living One" is his name,

"Righteousness" is her name. I live with my two children, I live with my two fledgelings, for I am in the midst of them, both of them follow after my body, and I lie down and live with my daughter Maat; one within me and one behind me, I stand up because of them both, their arms being about me. It is my son who will live, whom I begot in my name. He knows how to nourish him who is in the egg in the womb for me, namely the human beings who came forth from my eye which I sent out while I was alone with Nu in lassitude, and I could find no place on which to stand or sit, when On had not yet been founded that I might dwell in it, when my throne had not yet been put together that I might sit on it; before I had made Nut that she might be above me, before the first generation had been born, before the Primeval Ennead had come into being that they might dwell with me.

—Coffin Texts, *spell 80, translation by R. O. Faulkner.*

Closing

Protection is in Shu, the great ones rejoice, those who are in the Presence are content. Not to stir up fighting in On, for they have seen Shu bearing the mace; he leads appearance in glory to him whom he wishes, he grants length of time to the Enneads; he mixes the voices of those who are to come; he divides the hours and the dawns; he makes Ra content with Right, and Shu, the father of the gods, appears in glory with the river behind him in the flame of the sunshine.

—Coffin Texts, *spell 554, translation by R. O. Faulkner.*

All of the deities we have examined so far may be regarded as forms of the Supreme Being, the godhead or Creator, that is the highest concept of Deity, regarded as male, female, or androgynous. Now that we come to Shu, a slightly different concept is being expressed, for as we have seen, Shu belongs to the first generation of deities that emanates from, or has been created by, that Supreme Being. Although he is still a form of that Being, it may be thought that he does not possess the entirety of qualities that belong to the creator deity. Shu is the male aspect, the father of the gods, as it says in the closing prayer above. Karl W. Luckert, in *Egyptian Light and Hebrew Fire* (1991, p. 49), describes Shu as "the masculine 'phallus-semen-life-breath' extension of Atum." He is Atum's breath of life, the air or atmosphere, and the radiant light of the sun that shines through the atmosphere.

The description of Shu in the invocation shows him to have much in common with Ra-Atum himself and with Sekhmet, sailing in the solar boat and fighting off the serpent fiend, here called Nekau. Shu and Tefnut, like Sekhmet, are leonine deities. As twin lions, they are called Ruti, the guardians of the eastern and western horizons where the sun rises and sets. The chief center for their worship was at Leontopolis (City of the Lion), called Nay-ta-hut by the Egyptians, which was near to Heliopolis. Shu is also represented as a man with a feather on his head. He is often depicted separating his children, Nut and Geb, by holding his daughter Nut, the sky, above his head on his raised arms. As the atmosphere between earth and sky, Shu must take this role, even though the parting of the two lovers introduces another instance of suffering and misunderstanding inherent in creation. This separation first occurred when Shu and Tefnut were carried away in the waters of Nun, and then again when Atum was separated from his Eye and grew a replacement for her. Shu's act of separating the sky from the earth forms the space in which Ra-Atum's myriad manifestations as Khepera, coming into being as all the forms of life on earth, are able to take place. Shu as the air, Atum's breath of life, sustains all these forms of life. Thus we see, in the text chosen for Shu's reply above, he is called "Living One."

Karl Luckert, in the same book (p. 201), also suggests that the concept of four elements—earth, air, fire, and water—which is found in Greek philosophy, was derived from Egyptian cosmogony. Atum, he says, in his form as the primeval mound, is earth, Shu is air, Ra is fire, and water is represented by the Nun. Interestingly, this pattern can be seen occurring again in subsequent generations, with Tefnut as moisture, Geb as earth, Nut as sky, and Horus, incarnate in the pharaoh, as fire. It might also be argued that Osiris, as a form of the sun god, could represent the element of fire in the fourth generation. The four elements are not elements in the modern sense of the term, but are three forms that matter takes—solid, liquid, and gaseous—plus energy, comprising the constituents of the physical universe. The idea of the godhead being composed of a trinity identified with fire, air, and water is also found in the Jewish mystical system of the Cabala, though here the elements appear in a different order: Kether, the highest Sephirah on the Tree of Life, is associated with breath or air; the second, Chokmah (the male principle), is associated with water; the third, Binah (the female principle), is associated with fire (Kaplan, 1990, pp. 68–78). Although no direct influence of Egyptian religion on the Cabala can be proven, it is possible that philosophical traditions and mystery religions originating in the early centuries AD, in the Greek city of Alexandria in Egypt—where there was a large cosmopolitan intellectual community of Greeks, Egyptians, and Jews—could have been passed down to influence Jews of later centuries when the Cabala was developed. It was this rich social environment that gave rise to Neoplatonism and the writings of the *Hermetica* (Scott, 1993, translation of the original by Hermes Trismegistus) and stimulated the growth of mystery cults based on the cult of Osiris, as well as providing a foundation for the new religion of Christianity. Egyptian religious concepts influenced all these developments to one degree or another.

In the text chosen for the invocation above, it is said that Shu conducts the Eye goddess. As we have seen, this Eye is Hathor, Sekhmet, or Bast, but it can also be Tefnut. As already mentioned in the chapter on Hathor, in one version of the legend of the Eye leaving Egypt and going to Nubia, Shu, along with Thoth, enticed her back again. In the chapter on Thoth, we mentioned that Thoth and Shu could be regarded as similar deities, Thoth as an aspect of the Creator as Ptah, and Shu as an aspect of the Creator as Ra-Atum, and that consequently their consorts, Maat and Tefnut, could also be identified with one another. It should also be noted that in Shu's reply above, the name of Tefnut is said to be Righteousness. That is to say, Tefnut is indeed identified with Maat. This principle of Maat thus occurs in all three cosmogonies of Heliopolis, Hermopolis, and Memphis. Furthermore, in the Heliopolitan cosmogony she occurs in two generations. She is the platform on which the Creator, as Ra-Atum and Ptah, stands, she is the wife of Thoth, and, as Tefnut, she is the wife of Shu.

What we see here is that, in ancient Egyptian theology and mythology, the same ideas are expressed again and again in different myths and various contexts. This is why it is not possible to identify the deities as individual members, each with a distinct function, of a pantheon, as there is so much overlap. Not only are there parallels between the cosmogonies of various cult centers, but this repetition of concepts also conforms to the hermetic dictum "as above, so below," in that the divine cosmic pattern that appears at one level of creation, appears again at another level, and indeed in all situations. The same themes and relationships recur in various Egyptian myths: male and female pairs; relationships between mother, father, daughter, son; principles of earth, air, fire, and water; love and union; anger and conflict; separation and reunion; balance and wholeness. These concepts are used to describe the fundamental nature of the Divine, the order of the universe from the cosmic to the human level, and the human relationship with the Divine. It is important to recognize that this is not simply the crude mythology of a pre-scientific culture long dead trying to explain natural phenomena in anthropomorphic terms. These ideas, expressed in a symbolic and metaphorical way, constitute a spiritual and religious system that can still be relevant to people today.

TEN

MAAT

Invocation

Praise to you, Maat, daughter of Ra,
  consort of god, whom Ptah loves,
The one who adorns the breast of Thoth, who
    fashioned her own nature,
    foremost of the Souls of Heliopolis;
Who pacified the two falcon gods through her
    good will,
    filled the Per-wer shrine with life and dominion;
Skilled one who brought forth the gods from herself
    and brought low the heads of the enemies;

Who herself provides for the House of the All-Lord,
   brings daily offerings for those who are on duty.
Magnificent her throne before the judges—
   and she consumes the enemies of Atum.

—*Hymn to Maat in the Temple of Amun at el-Hibis, translation by
John L. Foster, in* Hymns, Prayers, and Songs: An Anthology of
Ancient Egyptian Lyric Poetry, *pp. 122–3.*

This is the path of Thoth to the House of Maat, and I will
be in the suite of Thoth at night, assembling them. I possess
Maat, I detest darkness, I open up the night. Fire.

I have come into the sky of the Double Lion, I have nurtured Maat. . . . Prepare a path for me that I may pass on it, that I may set Maat aright, and that I may split open the darkness.

—Coffin Texts, *spells 1093 and 1105, translation by R. O. Faulkner.*

Reply

Shout! I have taken the bark of acclamation. Shout! I have fashioned the bark of acclamation. I have ascended to the upper sky, and I have fashioned Nekhbet; I have descended to the lower sky of Ra, and I have fashioned Sekhmet. I have power in the shrine, for I have nourished Ra; I have traversed the middle sky . . . because I am Maat in these manifestations of hers which are upon and in the middle of Nekhbet, the entire Vulture. Her wings are opened to me, and Ra lives thereby every day. . . . Nekhbet has installed me in the midst of herself, because what is disliked is that Set should see me when I reappear.

. . . I am that Maat who is in the midst of Nekhbet, who loves Ra, Mistress of eternity, Mistress of the limits of sky and earth . . .

—Coffin Texts, *spell 957, translation by R. O. Faulkner.*

As already explained, Maat is the female principle of order in the universe. In the text chosen for the invocation, she is clearly an aspect of the Creator, in that she "fashioned her own nature" and "brought forth the gods." Her familiar role is presiding over the judges in the Hall of Judgment. Representing an abstract principle of order and justice, she "adorns the breast" of Thoth, her husband, almost as if he is wearing a pendant in the form of the goddess (which Egyptian judges may have worn as a symbol of office). Perhaps also "adorns the breast" alludes to a loving embrace between husband and wife. Here, however, she is also described as the "daughter of Ra and consort of god"—in this context "god" seems to refer to both Ra and Ptah. As we have seen, Ra has two daughters, Hathor-Sekhmet and Tefnut. In the chapter on Hathor, we quoted a text that describes Hathor like Maat, as the creator of law; but here, the reference describes Maat like Sekhmet—Maat "consumes the enemies of Atum," which is the role of Sekhmet the destroyer, consort of Ptah. As pacifier of the "two falcon gods," probably Horus and Set, Maat is the female counterpart of Thoth.

As mentioned in the previous chapter, there is evidence that Maat is identified with Tefnut, for spell 80 in the *Coffin Texts* says of Tefnut, "Righteousness is her name." The concept of Maat involves righteousness, justice, truth, balance, and order. As also mentioned before, Maat's consort, Thoth, is associated with Shu, the consort of Tefnut. This has resulted in Maat and Tefnut also becoming identified with one another. Maat is depicted as a young woman wearing a feather on her head—the female equivalent of Shu, who also wears a feather—but it seems that she was regarded more as an abstract principle than a goddess. Karl W. Luckert, in *Egyptian Light and Hebrew Fire* (1991, p. 50), explains that the idea of the godhead being a trinity of Atum, Shu, and Tefnut-Maat was later adapted by the Greek philosopher Plotinus, and at the same time a similar trinity was taken up by the Christians, expressed as Father, corresponding to Atum; Son, Christ in place of Shu; and Holy Spirit, corresponding to the Egyptian idea of Tefnut or Maat.

In the Heliopolitan cosmogony, Tefnut (pronounced "Tefnoot") is the female principle in the first generation of Deity, in which the female is distinct from the male rather than being contained within an androgynous Being, and she can therefore be seen as the mother of the gods. She is also the goddess of atmospheric moisture. Maat, however, is a more difficult concept to understand. As we have seen in the chapter on Ra-Atum, Maat was there at the beginning as the foundation on which the Creator made the world, and in this sense she can be identified with the primeval mound or Benben Stone; so despite being an abstract principle she seems to have a very solid presence, reminiscent of an earth deity.

This ambiguity is reflected in the second text of the invocation above, where the Double Lion could refer both to the earth god Aker, or to Shu and Tefnut. Aker is portrayed as a lion with a head and forelegs at both ends of its body; Akeru is portrayed as lion twins. Although the Akeru twins are earth deities, they were identified with the atmosphere deity twins, Ruti, who are Shu and Tefnut. This identification of atmosphere with earth may seem bizarrely illogical, but the idea is borne out in the text of Maat's reply above, where she claims to be the "Mistress of the limits of sky and earth."

In the reply, Maat is associated with Nekhbet, the vulture goddess of Upper Egypt. The Per-wer shrine, mentioned in the first text of the invocation, was the national shrine of Upper Egypt and was therefore under the protection of Nekhbet. She was represented on the pharaoh's crown alongside Wadjet, the cobra goddess of Lower Egypt. Nekhbet could also be represented as a cobra. As we have seen, the cobra as the uraeus on the brow of the Creator or on the brow of his representative, the pharaoh, is the Eye goddess, the primeval feminine aspect of Deity, and the symbol of the divine power of the Creator. Wadjet and Nekhbet together are the Two Ladies, the tutelary goddesses of the Two Lands of Egypt.

To the modern reader, all this is confusing, especially if we are trying to understand it in the misguided terms of a simple pantheon of deities. It is, however, typical of the ancient Egyptian mode of religious thought, where everything emanates from the one Deity and will eventually return to the Source. According to this way of thinking, the earth and the atmosphere are indeed different forms of manifestation of the same Supreme Being. If we are thinking in simplistic, literalist terms, we may well ask: How can Maat be the foundation on which Atum is standing, at the same time as being his spittle which forms Tefnut? This question reveals the wrongness of this literalist way of thinking, for the question can only be answered by taking a symbolic approach, which is closer to the mentality of the ancient Egyptian priesthood.

This symbolic approach is necessary to truly under-stand the connection between Maat and Tefnut in the sec-ond text of the invocation above. The text mentions fire and in referring to the Double Lion, alludes to the air and moisture of the Ruti. By implication (the Ruti being identi-fied with Aker), the text also refers to the earth element of Aker. Thus all four elements that make up the material world and sustain life are acknowledged in this text. There is even a hidden allusion to the passage of time here, as the Double Lion, the Akeru (the lions of Yesterday and Today), are guarding the western horizon at sunset and the eastern horizon at dawn. Since the text is about Maat, somehow all this must refer to her (and to Tefnut, who is identified with her); and it does, if we understand that Maat sustains all life and is the abstract and moral principle which is the foundation of the world. Order, justice, truth, and right-eousness, represented by Maat, are the underlying basis of creation, just as, on a physical level, the material elements represented by Tefnut are the underlying basis of creation. (To summarize what has been explained earlier, Tefnut rep-resents the physical elements as goddess of air and mois-ture, and as the element of earth in her form of Ruti or Aker, and as fire, implied by her lioness imagery and by the reference to fire in the second text of the invocation above.)

The second text of the invocation above also says that the path of Thoth, the god of wisdom and learning, leads to the house of Maat, and it is implied that possessing Maat dispels darkness. Again, this can only be understood symbolically: wisdom and learning lead to intellectual and moral enlightenment and to righteous behavior, justice, and orderliness. This is as much a part of the divine plan as the physical composition of the universe, arranged by Deity at the dawn of creation. For the ancient Egyptians, following this "path of Thoth," both through life and as a soul after death, was the way back to godhead.

The importance of Maat as the sustainer of the universe is essential to understanding her. In spell 80 of the *Coffin Texts*, Nu, the god of the Nun and "father" of Atum, instructs Atum to eat his daughter Maat. This must not be interpreted literally as cannibalism. Rather, Maat, as the principle of justice, order and truth, is the "food" of the gods, and Ra-Atum, the Supreme Being, lives entirely by this principle. As the nourishment and sustenance of the gods, Maat was offered to the main gods in their temple rituals, along with the other offerings of food, drink, and incense. In Amun's temple at Karnak, Maat was presented to Amun, Ra-Harakhti, and Ptah. She could also be offered to Thoth, her spouse, who was a major deity; but some gods, such as Set and Montu (the god of war), were not regarded as suitable recipients. The principle that Maat stands for was applied by the ancient Egyptians to poetry, music, art, weighing, measuring, and counting, as well as to human behavior and social justice (Hornung, 1992, p. 139). Maat encapsulates the ideas of correct behavior, harmony, the law, and fairness toward those who are disadvantaged. At death, each human is judged according to the principle of Maat—the scales of Maat weigh each heart against her symbol, the ostrich feather—and anyone weighed down by sin fails the test and is denied entry into the blessed afterlife.

For the Egyptians, Maat was something that had to be promoted, taught, and upheld in all areas of life, although at times they expressed pessimism about whether it could really be actively encouraged in this way. Some people seem to abide by Maat and others do not, and perhaps nothing can be done to improve the situation. Maat is a divine gift from which humans benefit; presenting this gift back to Deity in temple offerings was a way of ensuring that there was enough of it, or her, to go around and that, by returning it to the Source, it would continue to circulate freely. This way of thinking is part of a general belief that the ancient Egyptians had about their relationship to Deity. They saw this relationship as reciprocal: Humans would honor the gods, make offerings in temples, and assist in maintaining the order of the universe, so long as the gods responded by supplying air, water, sunlight, good harvests, and good health, and continued answering the prayers of their supplicants. There was a tacit understanding that Deity and humans would cooperate. This arrangement was all part of the balance and harmony of Maat. According to some magical texts that have survived, the deities had been occasionally threatened with withdrawal of religious rites and offerings unless they would comply with the demands made in a spell. The magician was able to do this because he assumed the godform of a deity when working a spell and thus issued the threat as one god to another. The magician himself was therefore protected from any repercussions.

Sometimes it has been said that the Egyptian concept of Maat can be equated with the Hindu concept of karma, which concerns cause and effect in a moral context, but this is not strictly true. The law of karma is often cited as an explanation for bad luck or a reason why someone is in unfortunate circumstances. There is no suggestion of this idea in the Egyptian way of thinking. Poverty and misfortune would have been seen by the ancient Egyptians as signs of the absence of Maat. Misfortune was sometimes regarded as divine retribution, but was frequently attributed to the malicious intervention of demons or spirits of the dead. Human beings, in the Egyptian way of thinking, were created equal, and inequality was a social problem, not divine justice (as we see in the *Coffin Texts*, spell 1130, which we used in the god's reply in the chapter on Amun). Maat was venerated as a goddess with her own temples; her workings in the universe were seen not as retributive justice, but as evidence of the Creator's benevolence and the fundamental goodness of the universe.

ELEVEN

NUT

Invocation

O Nut! You became a spirit,
you waxed mighty in the belly of your mother Tefnut
   before you were born.
How mighty is your heart!
You stirred in the belly of your mother in your name of
   Nut,
you are indeed a daughter more powerful than her
   mother . . .
O Great One who has become the sky!
You have the mastery,
   you have filled every place with your beauty,

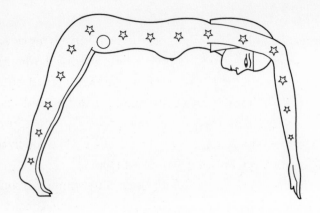

the whole earth lies beneath you, you have taken
 possession thereof,
you have enclosed the whole earth and everything
 therein within your arms. . . .
O high above the earth! You are supported upon your
 father Shu,
but you have power over him,
he so loved you that he placed himself—and all things
 beside—beneath you
so that you took up into you every god with his
 heavenly barque,
and as "a thousand souls is she" did you teach them
that they should not leave you—as the stars.

—Pyramid Texts, *utterances 427–434, in* Myth and Symbol in Ancient Egypt, *by R. T. Rundle Clark, pp. 48–9.*

Reply

Recitation by Nut, the greatly beneficent: [Osiris] is my eldest son who split open my womb; he is my beloved, with whom I am well pleased.... [Osiris] is my beloved son, my first-born upon the throne of Geb, with whom he is well pleased, and he has given to him his heritage in the presence of the Great Ennead. All the gods are in joy, and they say: How goodly is [Osiris]! His father Geb is pleased with him ...

Recitation by Nut: I enfold your beauty within this soul of mine for all life, permanence, dominion and health ...

I am your mother, I am Nut, and I have come so that I may enfold and protect you from all things evil.

—Pyramid Texts, *utterances 1, 3, and 11, translation by R. O.*
Faulkner, reprinted by permission of Oxford University Press.
Coffin Texts, spell 792, translation by R. O. Faulkner.

Nut (pronounced "Noot") or Nuit (pronounced "Noo-it") is a member of the Great Ennead of Heliopolis, the daughter of Shu and Tefnut. Her body is the night sky, the starry heavens; she is depicted as an elongated figure arched over the earth with her arms extended, fingertips touching the ground. Her name of "a thousand souls is she," used in the invocation above, evocatively expresses her nature as the abode of the stars, which are the gods and the souls of the justified dead. Stretched out, arms above her head, her image also decorates the inside of coffin lids as guardian of the dead. Sometimes she is depicted as a woman with a water jar on her head. (The hieroglyph for Nu is a water jar and this is also used as

the symbol for Nut, the *t* being a feminine ending on Egyptian words). She can also be represented as a cow, emphasiz-
ing her maternal qualities, and occasionally as a sow.

Nut is called Mother of the Gods and, as guardian of the
dead, the Great Protectress. In both roles she is essentially a
great mother goddess. She is mother of Osiris, Set, Isis,
Nephthys and, it is sometimes said, Horus the Elder. She is
also mother of the sun, Ra, to whom she gives birth each
morning and whom she swallows each night. The concept of
her as a sow who devours her own piglets represents this
idea, for she seems to give birth to and consume all the heavenly bodies that rise and set in her. The sun god was thought
to pass through the duat, or underworld, at night, but rather
than being under the earth, this region could be imagined as
being inside the body of the great mother, Nut. The ancient
Egyptians believed that Nut also granted the souls of the
dead a similar rebirth. She gave these souls options: to attend
Ra in his solar boat through the heavens, to join the company of the gods as stars in the mother's firmament, or to
"come forth by day" in any form they desired, including animals or plants, on Earth. The Greek concept of hades as a
murky underground realm, where the spirits of the dead had
a partial sort of existence, has given many people the impression that Pagans of the past had depressing ideas about the
afterlife. The ancient Hebrew notion of sheol, as described in
the book of Job (17:13–16), is no better—a gloomy pit
where the shades of the dead lose their faculties and eventually fade away. Christianity has tended to take credit for initi-
ating the concept of a blissful afterlife in the Divine presence

in a beautiful heavenly realm; but thousands of years earlier, it was the Egyptians who first conceived of the idea of "shining spirits" (souls of the justified dead) ascending to heaven to become one with the "imperishable stars" within the body of a loving mother goddess.

As we have already seen, there is evidence that the early Christians derived some of their ideas from the Egyptians. One of the more startling examples of this is in the text we have quoted above for Nut's reply. Her words in the first utterance of the *Pyramid Texts* will seem eerily familiar to anyone acquainted with the Christian tradition, for they are the same words spoken by a disembodied voice from heaven at the baptism of Jesus, when the Holy Spirit came down in the form of a dove (Matthew 2:16–17, Mark 1:9–11, Luke 3:21–22). Baptism is a symbolic form of spiritual rebirth; Jesus was baptized in Israel's sacred river, the Jordan. In non-patriarchal societies, a sacred river may be personified as a goddess, as is the Ganges in India. Egypt's sacred river, the Nile, is the earthly counterpart of what the Egyptians called the Winding Waterway (Milky Way) which also comprises part or all of the starry body of Nut. Barbara S. Lesko (1999, pp. 25–7) observes that Nut may have been regarded as the Milky Way, rather than the entire heavens. She presents an interesting theory that the myth of Nut's swallowing and then giving birth to the sun could derive from the sun's position in relation to the Milky Way in the pre–Dynastic Era (5500–3100 BC). At dawn on the spring equinox, the sun would have appeared at the "mouth" end, and on the morning of the winter solstice, it would have appeared at the "vagina" end, symbolizing, respectively, the conception and birth of the sun god. In Christian baptism, as well as in ancient Egyptian notions of rebirth in the afterlife, the reborn soul emerges from water, which symbolizes emerging from the amniotic fluid of the mother's womb, or, in cosmic terms, the primeval ocean. In Christian belief, the initiate is spiritually "born again" when he is physically immersed in water during a baptism ceremony. In Egyptian belief, the souls of the newly deceased bathed in the Field of Rushes. (Barbara Lesko, citing her husband L. H. Lesko, implies that the Field of Rushes is a region of heaven and may represent Nut's vulva.) As the newborn soul emerges, he is greeted by his divine mother, whether that be Nut or the Holy Spirit. The Holy Spirit is the Christian version of Tefnut, Nut's mother. As the primeval ocean, Nut is sometimes identified with Naunet, the female counterpart of Nu or the Nun.

Nut's consort, Geb, is of lesser importance in Egyptian religion compared to Nut. He may be only one of three sexual partners enjoyed by her, for, according to Plutarch ("Isis and Osiris"), only Set and Nephthys are Nut's children by Geb; the father of Osiris and Horus the Elder is Ra; and the father of Isis is Thoth. It was supposedly because of jealousy that Ra (who is both her grandfather and son, as well as being her lover!) cursed Nut with being unable to give birth on any day of the year, necessitating the intervention of her other lover, Thoth, to create the five epagomenal days on which her children could be born.

There is a myth in the Egyptian text called the *Book of the Divine Cow* that Ra lived as a king on Earth before the rebellion of mankind, when humans blasphemed against him on account of his apparently senile condition and he retaliated by sending his Eye, Sekhmet, to punish them. According to this story, after these events, Ra felt so tired and disillusioned that he could not bear to live on Earth any more; so he climbed onto the back of his mother Nut, who took the form of a great cow, and Nut's legs grew longer and longer as her body rose up into the sky. Some people, dismayed to see the sun departing, tried to persuade him to stay by taking up arms against the blasphemers, but the only consequence of this was to bring about the first occurrence of warfare. Ra declined to change his plans, giving Thoth extra divine powers, appointing him as his minister, the moon god, with the authority to punish the wrongdoers. This strange story, which on one level describes the coming of night, could also be regarded as an ancient Egyptian version of the Fall—an account of the separation of heaven and Earth and the reason why the gods no longer live among humans. This is a variation on themes we have addressed before: Ra-Atum's loss of his children and the misunderstanding with his errant Eye; the forcible separation of Nut and Geb by their father, Shu; and now this tale of Ra's withdrawal from sinful humanity on the back of Nut. These events all speak of the pain of separation and the inevitable loss of innocence as creation evolves, as Khepera comes into being in the forms of all the things that come into being, as the Lord of All unfolds the coils of the primeval serpent and passes millions of years between himself and Osiris, the son of Nut.

For the ancient Egyptian, however, separation from the Divine Source was only a temporary condition for those living on Earth. Much as the Egyptians loved life and lived it to the fullest, they also believed that death was the beginning of the journey back to godhead. As we shall see later, in the chapter on Osiris, by the time of the New Kingdom (1554–1075 BC), every virtuous dead person was identified with Osiris (a privilege once reserved for the pharaoh alone), so Nut came to be regarded as everyone's mother, and she would naturally welcome her beloved children into heaven. As nourisher of the blessed dead, Nut, like Hathor, is sometimes represented within a sycamore tree. In this form she provides the souls of the dead with air, water, and food.

Although Nut is a mother goddess in her own right and may originally have had a major cult of her own, she came to be regarded as one member of the Heliopolitan Ennead, and within this group of deities, as we have seen, the subsequent generations after Ra-Atum may be interpreted as emanations of the Supreme Being. Karl W. Luckert (1991, p. 321) speaks of the "Hand-Tefnut-Nut-Isis dimension of the Enneadean godhead." This means that the Hand of the Creator, like his Eye, is his feminine aspect; Just as the mighty power of his Eye, sometimes benign, sometimes destructive, manifests through Hathor or Sekhmet, his Hand also manifests as a goddess. As we shall later see, this goddess may be Tefnut, Nut, or Isis.

TWELVE

GEB

Invocation

O Geb, son of Shu . . . may your mother's heart quiver over you in your name of Geb, for you are the eldest son of Shu, his first-born.

O Geb . . . you are the sole great god. Atum has given you his heritage, he has given you the assembled Ennead, and Atum himself is with them, whom his eldest twin children joined to you; he sees you powerful, with your heart proud and yourself able in your name of "Clever Mouth," chiefest of the gods, you standing on the earth that you may govern at the head of the Ennead. Your fathers and

your mothers are pre-eminent among them, for you are mightier than any god. . . .

May you have power over the Ennead and all the gods . . . for you are the essence of all the gods. Fetch them to yourself, take them, nourish them . . . for you are a god having power over all the gods.

—Pyramid Texts, *utterance 592, translation by R. O. Faulkner,*
reprinted by permission of Oxford University Press.

Geb is the son of Shu and Tefnut and the husband of Nut. His name in older books is sometimes Seb, but this is no longer regarded as the proper form. He is the god of the earth, represented as a naked man with an erect phallus, lying on his back beneath the arched form of his much larger wife. He may also be represented as a goose, the hieroglyph of his name, or as a man with a goose on his head. In his goose form, Geb is the Great Cackler, a hermaphrodite deity who laid the Great Egg at the dawn of time from which the benu bird, or phoenix, was hatched.

In Western culture, we are so used to the concept of Mother Earth that it can seem somewhat strange that the ancient Egyptians regarded the earth deity as male. Part of the reason for this may be that, as we have already seen, from early in their civilization, their religious beliefs concentrated on a sun god who was born from a sky goddess (Hathor or Nut), and they had the idea that the dead were likewise reborn from this mother goddess in the sky. As a complement to this idea, the earth would be seen as male, unlike in cultures in which burial in the earth is seen as a return to the womb of the earth mother. In contrast, ancient Egyptian funerary texts speak of an earthquake and the earth being hacked up as the soul of a dead person ascends to the sky in triumph (*Pyramid Texts*, utterance 509). Also, as the cult of Osiris increased in importance, the myth of his death and resurrection, which relates to the seasonal vegetation cycle and the growth and harvesting of crops, would tend to reinforce the idea of the earth and its vegetation as male. Osiris's kingship is spoken of in terms of his having inherited the throne of Geb, which has the corresponding effect of establishing Geb as the forerunner of Osiris. Geb himself is sometimes represented with vegetation growing on his body, suggesting that he too can be regarded as a vegetation god.

The text used for the invocation above explains that Geb inherited his position from Atum, who could be regarded as his grandfather; but here care needs to be taken, for as Shu and Tefnut, the son and daughter of Atum, can perhaps more correctly be seen as expressions or forms of Atum himself, the same could be said of Geb. This is the sense in which Geb is the "sole great god," "chiefest of the gods," and "at the head of the Ennead," as it says in the text above. Also, as explained in part one, in a monolatrous religion, every god is regarded as the chief god and the sole god at the point of his worship. If understood in any other way, these terms are very misleading, for the importance of Geb in Egyptian religion derives from his role as a member of the Heliopolitan Ennead and not from his having any great significance as an individual deity. Just as Nut is mother of the gods, Geb is father of the gods; but for him this is really a title that he must share with Shu, for unlike Nut, whose importance tends to eclipse that of her mother, Geb does not stand out as a major deity in his own right.

The throne of Geb was of course the throne of Egypt and the inheritance of Geb was the right to rule as king, passed down through Osiris to his son Horus, who was incarnate in the reigning monarch. Therefore, any statement about Geb's throne or inheritance may be construed as a claim about the divine right of Egyptian kings. A pharaoh did not simply proclaim himself to be a god out of a sense of self-importance or delusions of grandeur; all his predecessors had been gods and he could trace his royal lineage back to the great gods who had ruled Egypt in prehistoric times. The ancient Egyptians would not have made the modern kind of distinction between myth and history, for their interpretation of history was mythologizing, and in particular they strove wherever possible to interpret events in terms of the Zep Tepi, the First Time, when gods were living on earth and the world was in a state of perfection. They had a strong desire that such a condition should be constantly renewed and that the world should be made to return to how it was in the First Time, when Maat prevailed.

A New Kingdom papyrus called the *Turin Royal Canon* lists the gods who ruled Egypt in pre–Dynastic times as Ptah, Ra, Shu, Geb, Osiris, Set, Horus, Thoth, and Maat, after whom came the demigods known as the Followers of Horus. The myth of how Geb succeeded his father Shu to the throne is inscribed on a black granite shrine that was built in Phakussa (Faqus), the capital of the twentieth nome of Lower Egypt, during the Ptolemaic Period (304–30 BC). The account describes how Shu, having been a good king who had overthrown the enemies of Atum and Ra, became weak toward the end of his long reign and was suffering from an eye disease. Geb became envious of his father's position as king and also began to desire his own mother, Tefnut. On the day that Shu and his retinue retired to heaven, Geb encountered his mother in the royal palace and raped her, thus in every sense taking his father's place. For nine days, the earth was subjected to total darkness and a howling wind. When environmental conditions returned to normal, Geb was found to have established himself on the throne and was accepted as the new king, taking the title Iry-paat-neteru, Heir of the Gods (Watterson, 1996, pp. 31–2, 36).

This story presents a rather unsavory image of Geb, but the morality of the gods is not necessarily that of human beings. As we have seen, their relationships, construed in human terms, would certainly be incestuous from the start with Hathor as both daughter and wife of Ra. Shu jealously separated Nut from Geb to create heaven and Earth, because, it is implied, he desired his daughter Nut for himself. Now Geb retaliates by claiming Shu's wife as his own, even though she is his mother. Once again, the theme of the eye recurs: Shu's eye disease seems symbolic of the weakening of his power. In Egyptian mythology, as we know, the eye of a god represents his divine power, his health and potency, his right to rule, and his female consort, so it is no surprise that Shu should lose all these once he has trouble with his eyes. This story about Geb and his mother also relates to the custom of incest within Egyptian royal families. The fact that a number of pharaohs married their sisters led Egyptologists to believe for a while that the royal line was passed down exclusively on the female side of the family and that a new king was obliged to establish the legitimacy of his rule by marrying the daughter of the previous king's wife, who was often his own sister. A sufficient number of cases where this did not occur have now been discovered to show that this was not a regular rule, but a practice favored by some kings, perhaps because it was a way of emulating the divine brother-sister married couple, Isis and Osiris.

For the deities, it seems, incest not only with a sibling but with a parent is also acceptable, even if it involves violence, for Geb suffers no censure, his authority as earth god and father of the gods remains unchallenged, and the invocation above gives the strongest impression that his position was secured in an entirely respectable way. When trying to understand relationships within the Ennead, we must bear in mind that a son can always be seen as a manifestation of his father, and a daughter as a manifestation of her mother. They are all ultimately emanations of Ra-Atum.

Geb's reputation as Clever Mouth, mentioned in the invocation above, may derive from another story about him. In an account on the Shabaka Stone (which we mentioned in the chapter on Ptah), Geb judges between the two gods in the trial that takes place after Osiris's death, first dividing the Two Lands between them, giving Lower Egypt to Horus and Upper Egypt to Set, but then changing his mind and deciding in favor of Horus as king of a united Egypt. According to *The Contendings of Horus and Set*, it is not Geb but Ra-Atum who presides over the trial; but the Shabaka Stone version of the story, in which Geb is the judge, seems to allude to a myth about Geb dividing Egypt between his two heirs, rather than to the Osirian myth, according to which it was first Osiris who inherited Geb's throne, and the dispute between Set and his nephew Horus did not take place until after Set had already been king of both the north and south. In an older version of the myth of the feud, Horus and Set are brothers, rather than nephew and uncle.

We shall address this apparent inconsistency in later chapters on the two Horuses and Set.

Perhaps it is worth mentioning here that the concept of Egypt as the Two Lands has often been taken literally, with some Egyptologists speaking as if the feud between Horus and Set is a myth based on an actual historical conflict between two rulers or two sets of people in prehistoric times. However, as we have said before, there is always a danger in interpreting myth too literally. In all the myths we have looked at so far, it is apparent that duality was a fundamental concept within the ancient Egyptian way of thinking: the distinction between one thing and another, and the relationships between different things—male and female, life and death, love and conflict or separation—are aspects of common experience necessary to life, and the ancient Egyptians were very much aware of this, as can be seen in their mythology. For them, creation began with division when Atum separated himself from the Nun, and separated his children from himself and from one another, and his Eye from his own face. For the Egyptians, to join two things together to make them one would therefore be to return to the undifferentiated unity of the First Time, to that primordial divine state before any division had taken place. In this metaphysical sense, rather than a literal sense, Egypt, and indeed the whole Earth, can be seen as the Two Lands, for this is the realm of separation and conflict; day-to-day life is experienced in this dualistic way. Therefore, when Geb divides Egypt into Two Lands under Horus and Set, he creates the conditions for life on Earth; but the ideal state is when the Two Lands are united under Horus, the incarnation on Earth, in the form of the pharaoh, of the sun god and Creator, Ra. It was the duty of each pharaoh to be the Horus for his people, bringing order, peace, and prosperity under his rule. In this way the Two Lands are one, but at the same time they remain two, because duality is a necessary condition for existence.

THIRTEEN

OSIRIS

Invocation

Homage to thee, Osiris, lord of eternity, king of the gods, many of names, holy of creations, hidden of forms in temples, whose ka is venerated. Chief of Djedu, great one contained in the temple of Sekhem, lord of praises in Athi, chief of the sacred food in Heliopolis, the lord who is commemorated in the place of the Maati. Hidden soul, lord of Qerert, holy one in White Wall, ba of Ra, of his very body. Satisfied with offerings in Suten-Henen, abundant of praise in the naret-tree, his ba hath become exalted as lord of the great house in Khemennu. Great one of terror in Shas-hetep, lord

of eternity, chief of Abydos. His seat extendeth in the land of holiness, established of name in the mouth of mankind, the companies of the Two Lands. Tem, the divine god of the kas, chief of the company of the gods, spirit beneficent among the spirits. He draweth from Nu his waters, he bringeth along the wind of eventide and air to his nostrils, to the satisfaction of his heart.

His heart germinateth, he produceth the light, the divine food. Heaven and the stars obey him, he maketh to be open the great gates. Lord of praises in the southern heaven, adored in the northern heaven, the stars which never diminish are under the seat of his face. His seats are the stars which never rest. Cometh to him an offering by the order of Geb, the company of the gods praise him, the stars of the duat kiss the earth before him, the boundaries of earth bow down, the limits of heaven make supplication when they see him. Those who are among the holy ones fear him, the Two Lands, all give to him praises in meeting his majesty, the glorious master, chief of masters, endowed with divine rank, established of dominion.

Beautiful form of the company of the gods, gracious of face, beloved by him that seeth him. He putteth his awe in all lands, through love of him they all proclaim his name before every name. All make offerings to him, the lord who is commemorated in heaven and in earth, greatly praised in the Wag festival. The Two Lands together make to him cries of joy, the great one, first of his divine brethren, prince of the company of the gods, establisher of Maat throughout the Two Lands, placer of the son upon the great throne of his father Geb, darling of his mother Nut, great one of two-fold strength; he casts down Seba, he hath slaughtered his enemy, placing his fear in his foe. . . .

Heir of Geb and the sovereignty of the Two Lands. He hath seen his power, he hath given to him command to lead the lands by his hand to the end of times. He hath made this earth by his hand, its waters, its air, its green herbs, all its cattle, all its birds, all its fishes, its reptiles, its quadrupeds. The desert belongs by right to the son of Nut, the Two Lands are content to crown him on the throne of his father like Ra. He riseth on the horizon, he giveth light through the darkness, he shineth with light from his plumes, he floodeth with light the Two Lands like Aten at the early sunrise. His crown pierceth heaven, he is a brother of the stars, the guide of every god, operative by command and word, favored one of the great company of the gods, beloved of the little company of the gods.

—*An Eighteenth Dynasty Hymn to Osiris, based on the transliteration by E. A. Wallis Budge, in* The Gods of the Egyptians, *Vol. II, pp. 162–8.*

Reply

I am Osiris, the brother of Isis. My divine son, together with his mother Isis, hath avenged me on mine enemies. My enemies have wrought every kind of evil, therefore their arms, and hands, and feet, have been fettered by reason for their wickedness which they have wrought upon me. I am Osiris, the first-born of the divine womb, the first-born of the gods, and the heir of my father Osiris-Geb. I am Osiris, the lord of the heads that live, mighty of breast and powerful of back, with a phallus which goeth to the remotest limits where men and women live. I am [Orion] who traveleth over his domain and who journeyeth along before the stars of heaven, which is the belly of my mother Nut; she conceiveth me through her love, and she gave birth to me because it was her will so to do.

—Book of the Dead, *chapter 69, translation by E. A. Wallis Budge.*

Come in peace . . . so says Osiris. You shall see me in my great atef crowns which Ra gave to me and which Atum and the Enneads made firm for me, being pleased about it. You shall see me . . . with my uraei on my brow and my atef

crowns on my head, my staff in my grasp and my knife in
my grip, my image of Truth on my shoulder, and crooked-
ness under my feet. I confirm powers, I promote positions,
I obstruct my foes who shall come opposing me, because I
have appeared as ruler of the sky and king of the earth, and
my foes fall through fear when they see me. I am exalted in
my great atef-crowns which are in Ninsu, and I indeed am
your father, O my offspring upon earth.

   —Coffin Texts, *spell 313, translation by R. O. Faulkner.*

Osiris (whose original Egyptian name is Asar or Ausar) is
the god of death and resurrection, whose principle abode is
the duat or underworld. The duat is an otherworldly realm,
the entrance to which is in the sky, at the horizon. In the
Heliopolitan cosmogony, Osiris is the first-born child of
Nut, belonging to the third generation of deities after Ra-
Atum. This position, however, belies his importance as a
major deity of ancient Egypt, his strong popular following,
and his stature of great importance in the mythology at-
tached to kingship. He has a significant role in the *Pyramid
Texts*, the oldest religious writings (c. 2345 BC), and arche-
ological evidence relating to him has been found that dates
from earlier than this. Although, as we have repeatedly
seen, any one of the major Egyptian deities could stand for
the Supreme Being, or be called the greatest god or chief of
the gods, this is true of some deities more than others and
in particular it applies to Ra-Atum, Ptah, Amun, and
Osiris. The importance of Osiris in this respect is very apparent in the text that we have chosen for the invocation

above, which is part of a long hymn giving an account of the Osirian myth.

Osiris is typically represented as a mummiform man with green or black skin, wearing the plumed atef crown, holding his insignia of crook and flail, and standing on the plinth, which represents Maat. He is often accompanied by his wife Isis and sister Nephthys. His main cult centers were at Busiris (Djedu or Andjet), where he took over the identity of Andjety, a god already worshipped there, and at Abydos (Abdu), where he likewise assumed the identity of Khentimentiu, a falcon god of the dead. The tomb of King Djer of the First Dynasty, located in a royal cemetery outside Abydos, was believed by the ancient Egyptians to be the tomb of Osiris. Many thousands of pilgrims visiting the site left pots containing food offerings, with the result that the area became strewn with so many pots that it is known today as Umm el-Qa'ab, meaning "Mother of Pots." In the invocation above, some place names for Osiris's other centers of worship are mentioned, which may be unfamiliar: Athi is the ninth nome of Lower Egypt; White Wall (Ineb-hedj) is Memphis; and Qerert is Elephantine.

Osiris's name has been interpreted variously as meaning "seat-maker," "place of the eye," and "Mighty One," among other possibilities. The name is written with the hieroglyphs of the eye and the throne, which relate to divine power and kingship, respectively.

The myth of Osiris accrued its many features over the centuries. Egyptian sources contain fragments of the myth, but there is no surviving Egyptian text that recounts the whole story as a continuous narrative. For the full story, we rely on accounts given by classical writers in the first to second centuries AD. It is recounted that Osiris and Isis were king and queen of Egypt in ancient times. Under the rule of Osiris, the people were brought out of a condition of barbarity, trained in agricultural techniques, and given a system of laws and an organized religion. Osiris traveled abroad to spread his message of peaceful, civilized living. According to Diodorus (*Library of History,* 1.18), he was accompanied by a colorful band of singers, dancers, musicians, and satyrs, and traveled as far as India, where he founded Nysa and other cities. Meanwhile, Isis governed Egypt in his absence. Motivated by jealousy, which was perhaps aggravated by an illicit affair between Osiris and Set's wife Nephthys, his brother Set murdered Osiris upon his return to Egypt and threw his body into the Nile. Either Osiris was twenty-eight or it was the twenty-eighth year of his reign when this occurred. The site of the murder, close to Abydos, is referred to in Egyptian texts as Nedit, meaning "where he was cast down" (*Pyramid Texts,* utterances 442, 532, 576). In the *Coffin Texts,* spell 837, Nedit is said to be in the land of Gehesty. Egyptian sources say that Set committed the murder while he was in the form of an animal, an ox or a wild bull (*Pyramid Texts,* utterance 670).

Plutarch provides an embellished account of the murder, in which Set, on the pretext of playing a party game and with the help of seventy-two guests at a welcoming home party, tricks Osiris into climbing into an ornate box (perhaps a coffin or mummy case), that has been made to the exact dimensions of his body, and which is then sealed and thrown into the Nile by Set and his accomplices.

The body of Osiris traveled downstream and was washed onto the bank, where a tree (the naret-tree mentioned in the invocation above), said to be a cedar, acacia, tamarisk, or erica (heather), grew up around it. This is referred to in the *Pyramid Texts*, utterance 574, which also mentions the Djed-pillar—a fertility fetish known as the "backbone of Osiris," which was erected in a winter festival each year and was supposed to be a stylized representation of the tree. Egyptian texts also tell of the body being found and brought to the bank by Isis and Nephthys (*Pyramid Texts*, utterance 694). According to Plutarch, the body of Osiris in the box was washed as far as Byblos in Syria. The tree that grew around it was later cut down and incorporated as a pillar into the fabric of the palace of the king and queen of that country, but was eventually recovered by Isis. There is probably a misinterpretation of the word *byblos*, which means "book" and could be used to refer to papyrus. With this in mind, the papyrus swamps of the delta region of Egypt may have been originally indicated, rather than the city in Syria.

After Isis recovered the body, she hid it, but Set discovered it, dismembered it (into fourteen pieces, according to Plutarch, or twenty-six, according to Diodorus), and scattered the parts across Egypt. Isis went in search of the pieces and at each place where she found one, she established a temple for the worship of Osiris. Egyptian texts indicate that Nephthys, Anubis (the son of Nephthys and Osiris), and Horus (an older son of Isis and Osiris, or their brother Haroeris), were also involved in the recovery of the body and the resurrection of Osiris. This story of the scattering of his dismembered body parts seems to have been devised to account for why several cult centers claimed to be the god's burial place. However, Isis is said to have buried only replicas of the body parts, for she reassembled Osiris's body and then brought him back to life by means of magic. They managed to conceive their son, Horus the Younger, called Harpocrates or Harsiese (*Pyramid Texts*, utterance 366). Alternatively, this resurrection may have occurred before Set dismembered the body. It is also said that when the body was dismembered, the phallus was missing, because Set had thrown it into the Nile, where it was eaten by a fish, so Isis was obliged to make a replacement.

After his death, Osiris descended to the underworld, which was a place of darkness. This event is described in the *Book of the Dead*, chapter 175, where he calls out to Atum for an explanation of where he is and what is going to happen to him. Atum replies that Osiris will live for millions of years, while his son Horus rules from his throne on Earth, until the time comes when Atum will destroy the world and only he and Osiris will remain, taking the form of serpents. This theme is significant, and we shall return to it shortly. Later, after his resurrection, Osiris ascended to heaven as the constellation of Orion, as mentioned in the first text of the god's reply above. (See also *Pyramid Texts*, utterance 442.) His appearing as Orion was celebrated annually during the Wag festival in early August, referred to in the invocation above.

This myth of Osiris is very important in understanding the deeper aspects of Egyptian religion. The Mysteries of Osiris, in the form of the Graeco–Roman cult of Isianism, spread throughout the known world, even as far as the north of England. The Graeco–Roman form of Osiris is Sarapis, a combination of Osiris and the Apis bull, an animal sacred to Ptah and Osiris. Sarapis is portrayed as a bearded, mature man, and was conceived similarly to Dionysus and other Greek gods. It is generally accepted by scholars that Isianism and its myth of the death and resurrection of Osiris had an effect upon the development of Christianity. Just how profound an effect that might have been has been demonstrated by Timothy Freke and Peter Gandy in their most interesting book, *The Jesus Mysteries*, in which they argue that Christianity is based entirely upon the Mysteries of Osiris and its Greek offshoot, the Mysteries of Eleusis. When these Pagan elements in Christianity are set aside, virtually no evidence remains of Jesus as an actual historical figure. It follows from this that the mystical teachings of Christianity found in Gnosticism and in the letters of Saint Paul in the New Testament are a Jewish interpretation of teachings in the Egyptian and Greek Mysteries and that Christianity is essentially a Jewish version of the same religious ideas.

The similarities are very clear: Osiris, like Jesus, is a "son of God" who is incarnated on Earth with a mission to spread a moral message to reform a corrupt society; like Jesus, who is betrayed to his enemies by Judas, a "brother" disciple, Osiris is betrayed by his brother who conspires with a group of people to bring about his death; and just as Jesus suffers and dies on a cross or post, often referred to as a "tree," so does Osiris suffer and die within the tree that grows up around him, represented symbolically by the Djed-pillar. A tradition about Jesus based on an interpretation of Ephesians 4:7–9 claims that he "harrowed hell" (rescued the sinners who were there) during the two days that he was dead, before his resurrection from the tomb and encounter with Mary Magdalene (said to be his wife, according to a heretical tradition), which was followed later by his ascension to heaven. Similarly, Osiris descends to the underworld, is resurrected by his wife Isis with whom he has a sexual encounter before he ascends to heaven. Jesus is called the Savior of the World and his birth was heralded by portents and prophesies; but according to Plutarch, Osiris's birth was similarly accompanied by a prophesy from the shrine of Zeus (Amun) and a mysterious voice declaring, "The Lord of All advances to the light" ("Isis and Osiris," in *Moralia*, 355e). Jesus is the Good Shepherd, and his bishops today still carry a crook as a sign of their office; but thousands of years earlier, Osiris had the title Unnefer, the "good being," and carried a shepherd's crook as part of his insignia. Long before Jesus, it was Osiris who was called King of Kings, Lord of Lords, and Prince of Peace, and it was Osiris who presided over the Last Judgment of the souls of the dead.

Aspects of the myth of Osiris seem to allude to beliefs found in the practice of shamanism as well. The sacred tree, the descent to the underworld and ascent to heaven, and the theme of dismemberment are all characteristic of shamanic experience.

The myth can be interpreted on two levels. The exoteric interpretation is that Osiris is a vegetation god who manifests in trees and crops, dies each year at the harvest, and is reborn when the new seed grows. Furthermore, he is the moon that is "dismembered" by losing a fourteenth part on each of the fourteen days of its waning, and is restored to completeness during its waxing period. In recognition of this, the Egyptians performed rites in honor of Osiris on the first and the fifteenth day of each month to mark the appearance of the new moon and the full moon.

On an esoteric level, however, Osiris may be regarded as the divine part of the soul of every person that is incarnate in a human body, works, suffers, and dies on Earth, and is resurrected in the heavenly afterlife through the love and magical powers of the gods. Members of the Christian Church collectively comprise the "body" of Christ on Earth (1 Corinthians 6:15). The followers of Osiris could claim the same of their god. The body of Osiris, in the form of thousands of people, is scattered across the earth. As we have seen in Egyptian belief, everything that has come into being as an emanation of the creator god, Ra-Atum manifesting as Khepera, which takes its final form as the dismembered, scattered bodily parts of Osiris, will eventually return from where it has come. In the image of the primeval serpent Kematef uncoiling and coiling back upon itself, the Egyptians expressed this concept. In the *Book of the Dead*, chapter 175, this image becomes two serpents, Atum and Osiris, God as the first and the last, returning to the primal conditions of the waters of Nun. As in the symbol of the ouroboros, which is sometimes depicted as two snakes biting each others' tails, the end returns to the beginning.

By the time of the New Kingdom, every dead person was said to be "an osiris" and was "justified" or "true of voice," which meant that he or she had testified before Osiris in his Hall of Judgment and had been found worthy to enter his blessed realm. Osiris himself had been declared "true of voice" by Thoth in a tribunal of the gods after his resurrection. According to Egyptian texts, after this happened and Set was thereby discredited as a legitimate king, Osiris sat on Set, thus acquiring his name meaning "seat-maker" (*Pyramid Texts*, utterance 372; *Coffin Texts*, spell 577).

In the Graeco–Roman cult of Isianism, initiation involved an encounter with Osiris in the symbolic form of the sun shining at night, as described by Apuleius in *The Golden Ass* (a novel dating from the second century AD). It seems that the initiate would have been led through a number of chambers in which he was presented with various symbolic scenes, as the different parts of the ritual were performed and the mysteries were revealed to him. The basis of this symbol of the sun shining at night is that, during the night, Ra enters the underworld and is assimilated to Osiris, and in the morning he rises again (Griffiths, 1975, pp. 303–6). Osiris is called the *ba* of Ra, that is, the "soul" of Ra. Osiris's resurrection as Ra corresponds to the resurrection of the human soul as Osiris and consequently as Ra, providing an assurance that devotees of Isis and Osiris survive death and enjoy a blessed existence in another realm—a belief that is at the heart of the Mysteries of Osiris. The idea that the rebirth of the sun god and the resurrection of Osiris imply resurrection or rebirth for everyone makes sense only if there is some identification of the devotee with Deity, and as we have seen, the belief that everything and everyone partakes of the Divine is also a fundamental part of ancient Egyptian religion. In this sense, Osiris may be regarded as the higher self or as the divine spark in the soul of every person.

FOURTEEN

ISIS

Invocation

Hail to you, Lady of Goodness, at seeing whom those [who] are in the Netherworld rejoice, who removes the limpness of the Inert One, because of whom Osiris has trodden, who made for him the stride of those who walk in his moment of interment, in this your name of "Dam which is under the feet ..."

Hail to you, Mourner of Osiris who bewails the limp Great One; who makes a spirit of the Bull of the West; at seeing whom the Westerners rejoice; Lady of All in the Secret Place; to whom Osiris turns his back in these his moments of inertness; who is in front of the Lord of Abydos; whose

place on the paths of the Netherworld is hidden; who bewails her lord at the interment in this her name of "She who bewails her lord." . . .

Hail to you, Mourner of Osiris, Companion of the Bull of Nedit who makes the mummy-wrappings to breathe, who veils the limpness, to whom Osiris has turned his back, helper of the embalmer Anubis when treating the body of the Inert One. . . .

Hail to you, Great One behind your lord; who raises him up after being limp, who gathered [his] body together, who pulled [his] flesh together, who spiritualized [him], who split open [his] mouth for [him] . . .

Hail to you, you who are in attendance on your lord, Mourner of Osiris, the Great One, the Wailer, Mistress of the Per-nu . . .

Hail to you, Mistress of the Old Ones, Lady of many faces in the Secret Place, who gives orders to the Bull of Djedu, who guides the Lord of the West, at whom Osiris rejoiced when he saw her: Mistress of the hidden mysteries, who announces festivals in the bow of the bark when men navigate in the morning, to whom the Inert One has turned his face in this her name of Mistress of faces. . . .

Hail to you, Lady of offerings, at whom Osiris rejoices when he sees her, whose great wall is an owner of possessions; who brings air, who gives offerings, who presides over the throne in the secret places of the Netherworld; who clears the vision of the Bull of Djedu, who split open his mouth and split open his eyes when the Inert One asked; who gathered together his arms and legs, who laid Osiris down . . . who gave abundance to the Lord of the Flood on the desert plateau; who gave offerings.

She whose head was cut off with a knife.
She of the papyrus-plant whose milk is sweet.
She of vegetation which her lord divided.
She whom Horus examined . . .
Mistress of herbage who makes the Two Lands green.
Mistress of the night who takes possession of the Two
    Lands.

She who bent Set on account of her utterance.

She who cleared Horus's vision for him.

She who placed her lord in her embrace for herself.

I come that I may greet you, you Mourner of Osiris, who conceal the Great One from the flood of ill; Mistress of thrones who makes a spirit of the Bull of the West, at seeing whom the Westerners rejoice; Mistress of All in the secret places . . .

I come that I may greet you, O Great Lady who are behind your lord . . .

> —Coffin Texts, *spells 236–241, 828, and 993, translation by R. O. Faulkner.*

Reply

I am a net-snake, a soul in the bark "Ordainer of power." I am mistress of the oar in the Bark of Governance. I am the mistress of life, the serpent-guide of the sunshine on fair paths. I am she who strengthens the lashings on the steering-oars on the western ways. I am the third one, mistress of brightness, who guides the great ones who are languid on the paths of the wakeful. I am the mistress of splendor on the paths of the cloudy sky. I am mistress of the winds on the Island of Joy. I am the mistress of strength who guides those who are in their caverns. I am Hathor, mistress of the northern sky, who strengthened the bonds of the wakeful on that night when the earth quaked and seksut was among the mourners. I am Isis whom Nut bore, who displays her beauty, who puts together her power and who lifts up Ra to the Day-bark.

—Coffin Texts, *spell 332, translation by R. O. Faulkner.*

Closing

Isis, Creator of the universe,

Sovereign of the sky and stars,

Mistress of life,

Regent of the Gods,

Magician with divine wisdom,

Female sun,

Who stamps everything with her royal seal!

Man lives on your order,

Nothing happens without your agreement.

—*Inscription in the Temple of Isis at Philae, in* The Living Wisdom of Ancient Egypt, *by Christian Jacq, p. 109.*

Isis (the Greek name for Aset or Auset) is perhaps the greatest of all Egyptian goddesses, in that her worship endured for an inordinate period of time, outlasting the ancient Egyptian civilization itself, and spreading far beyond the land of Egypt. She has an important role in the *Pyramid Texts* as a guide and protector of the dead, showing that even from this time of the earliest religious writings, she was regarded as a major deity. In AD 331, the Emperor Constantine decreed that all Pagan temples be closed, as Christianity became the official religion of the Roman Empire, but the Temple of Isis at Philae managed to survive as a center of her worship until the sixth century. The Graeco–Roman religion of Isianism by that time had spread throughout the known world, from Egypt to the north of England, from Turkey to Portugal, and it proved very difficult to suppress. There is a sense in which it never really was suppressed, its appeal as a danger-ous rival to Christianity being turned eventually to the Church's advantage when Isianism was reinvented as the cult of the Virgin Mary, and statues of Isis became the inspiration for Black Madonnas in some parts of Europe, even to the ex-tent that some ancient statues may have been reused for this purpose. There is an account of a statue of the goddess long preserved in the church of St. Germain des Pres, until its true nature was recognized and it was destroyed as a Pagan idol (Witt, 1971, p. 274).

Isis is a member of the Great Ennead of Heliopolis. The eldest daughter of Nut and Geb, she was married to Osiris and was said to have lived with him on Earth as a queen of Egypt in ancient times. She is usually portrayed as a woman wearing on her head the vulture headdress and disc and horns of Hathor or the throne symbol, which is the hiero-glyph for her name. Sometimes she possesses long wings at-tached to her arms or she may be shown nursing her son Horus. The vulture headdress is indicative of her association with the goddess Mut, although Isis has her own bird form as a kite (a small bird of prey), in which aspect she is known as the Screecher, or the Wailer, as in the invocation above. From the New Kingdom, she became increasingly identi-fied with Hathor and eventually acquired the attributes of all the other major goddesses.

In the excerpts from the *Coffin Texts* chosen for the invocation above, the goddess is addressed with many titles, but not named as Isis, although the descriptions are so apt for Isis that she may well be the goddess intended. The title "Mistress of faces," meaning a goddess with numerous aspects, is certainly appropriate for Isis, who assimilated so many features and functions of other goddesses; and, as we will see later in this chapter, "Mistress of thrones" would seem to belong to Isis as well. Her name means "throne."

In the reply above, from spell 332, "third one, mistress of brightness," may refer to the star Sirius or Sothis, called Sopdet by the Egyptians, which was sacred to Isis. It is the brightest star (not including the planets) in the northern hemisphere, and its heliacal rise (just before dawn) in summer heralded the annual Nile flood and the new year in ancient Egypt. Sirius and Orion, representing Isis and Osiris, were absent from the night sky during the early summer, having disappeared after the harvest in the spring when Osiris died as god of the crops and vegetation. With the sun at its hottest, the land would become parched, plants and even animals would die, and the desert, the domain of Set, would start to encroach on the fertile land, signifying the reign of Set after murdering his brother. At about the time of the summer solstice, during the Pyramid Age, Sirius and Orion would reappear, symbolizing for the Egyptians that Isis had found the body of her husband; the flooding of the Nile, which followed, could be interpreted as her tears. After the flood had subsided, the next year's crops could be planted to grow through the winter, at which time the resurrection of Osiris would be celebrated —for us, this is the middle of November. Thus, for the ancient Egyptians, heavenly events corresponded to the seasonal crop cycle. Precession of the equinoxes means that the heliacal rise of Sirius now occurs in August and the damming of the Nile now prevents it from flooding.

The central role of Isis in the myth of Osiris has already been described in the previous chapter. Not only is she the main protagonist, but she provides the link between the story about the death and resurrection of Osiris and the battle between Horus and Set for the throne. This central role of Isis is hardly surprising, if we see Isis as the personification of the throne itself. The original Egyptian form of her name, Aset, written with a hieroglyph in the form of a throne, is thought to mean "throne" or "seat," suggesting that the goddess may have been identified with the throne. The child, Horus, sitting on the lap of his mother Isis was the image of the pharaoh, the earthly Horus, enthroned. He became king when, at his coronation, he sat for the first time as Horus on the lap of his mother, Isis the throne. As the throne, Isis literally made the king, just as in myth she makes Horus, not through normal biological methods, but by means of a profound act of magic. In the famous Eighteenth Dynasty hymn to Osiris, part of which is used as the invocation of Osiris in the previous chapter, a later verse describes how Isis, taking the form of a kite, flies around the land unceasingly until she finds her husband's body, and then, using her feathers or hair, makes a magical wind that fans into him the breath of life. She is able to arouse him sufficiently for them to achieve sexual union, and so conceives their son Horus. Even this may not be a natural act, for in the account by Plutarch ("Isis and Osiris"), Osiris's phallus is missing, so Isis has to fashion an artificial one. This may be a reference to the fact that male mummies were often provided with an artificial member, in case the real one suffered in the mummification process or was otherwise lost. In the funerary ceremonies for a dead pharaoh, the mummified king's symbolic union with Isis (the king having assumed the identity of Osiris and Isis being in her form of Sothis, the goddess of the star Sirius) may well have speeded the king's soul on the way to an afterlife in the constellation of Orion as well as have created the conditions for his heir to become the new Horus king.

The sufferings of Isis did not end with the resurrection of Osiris; while he went into the afterlife as the king of the dead, Isis was left on Earth as a pregnant widow, dispossessed by Set. In the *Coffin Texts*, spell 148, Isis, who in this alternative version of the myth seems to have been inseminated by a bolt of lightning, seeks help from Atum and the other gods in protecting her son "in the egg" before he is born. (The ancient Egyptian word for "egg" is the same as for "embryo.") Atum at first seems skeptical of her claim to be bearing the son of Osiris and of her prediction that this heir will kill Set and inherit the throne of Geb, but when she insists on the truth of what she is saying, he decrees that she will be hidden and agrees to grant magical protection.

Some of the stories about the subsequent problems encountered by Isis and the child Horus form the basis of ancient Egyptian healing spells (Borghouts, 1978). In one of these, we learn that Isis went into hiding from Set in the papyrus marshes of Khemmis or Chemmis. In the *Coffin Texts*, spell 286, Horus says that he was conceived in Pe and born in Chemmis. In a healing spell, Isis explains how she was imprisoned by Set in a spinning-house until Thoth rescued her and told her to take Horus into hiding in the marshes. In this particular spell, Isis is accompanied by seven scorpions that protect her, which would seem to associate her with Serket, the scorpion goddess (Borghouts, 1978, p. 59). The imprisonment by Set could mean that he enslaved Isis to work for him; but on the other hand, the fact that another spell mentions that Set's wife Nephthys was at the spinning-house too suggests that the place may simply be a house of women, Set's harem. In either case, his claim on the previous pharaoh's wife, who here embodies the throne itself, could be interpreted as a method for securing his own kingship.

Judging from the healing spells, Horus suffered many attacks from scorpions and snakes (emissaries of Set) while he was a child, and Isis had to use her magical powers on many occasions to save him from being poisoned by these stings and bites. In one spell, she is so distraught that she forgets the healing formula and appeals to heaven until the sun stops in the sky and Thoth leaves the company of the solar boat to come down to perform the healing magic on Horus (Borghouts, 1978, p. 65). Isis comes immediately to heal Horus on two occasions when he receives burns—once when he is in the desert and once when he has been left alone while Isis is in the spinning-house (Borghouts, 1978, pp. 24–6). Isis also heals him of a bout of indigestion from eating a sacred fish, and from migraines, of which he appears to be a frequent sufferer. Once, he and Thoth suffer from migraines at the same time and Horus begs Isis and Nephthys to give him one of their heads in exchange for his, as a cure (Borghouts, 1978, pp. 30–1 and 33).

Isis obtained her magical powers either from Thoth, who may have been her father, according to Plutarch, or by virtue of the secret magical name of Ra. One of the healing spells, which has become known as the Legend of Ra and Isis, describes how Isis makes a serpent of clay mixed with Ra's saliva and allows it to bite him. Ra becomes sick, and the only cure is to conjure the poison out of him by using his secret name, which is a word of power, so he is obliged to reveal the name to Isis in order for her to perform the spell that will heal him. It is implied in this story that the secret name is equated with the heart and the two eyes of Ra, which are the sun and the moon (Borghouts, 1978, pp. 51–5). Isis is allowed to share the power of this secret name with Horus, who was also regarded as a healing deity.

The serpent, as we know, is a goddess symbol, especially associated with Hathor and Sekhmet as the Eye of Ra, so it is significant that Isis uses this animal, which in a sense represents herself, in her attack on Ra. The goddess who speaks in spell 332 (*Coffin Texts*) used for the reply above, may be both Isis and Hathor as the serpent of power on the brow of Ra-Atum, the female aspect of the Supreme Being. (Incidentally, the meaning of the word *seksut*, which appears in this passage, is not known.) That Isis may be regarded as Ra-Atum's female aspect, his Eye, in any case is evident from her presence in the Heliopolitan Ennead, which makes her, like the other members of this company, an emanation of the Lord of All under a specific aspect. Further evidence of this is found in a healing spell in which Isis is the mother of Ra's offspring, Shu and Tefnut, rather than, as we might have expected, being their granddaughter (Borghouts, 1978, p. 40).

After Horus grows up, Isis encourages him to challenge Set for the throne. In *The Contendings of Horus and Set*, she causes so much trouble at a tribunal of the gods that Ra-Atum moves the meeting to an island and instructs the ferryman not to bring her across. Isis uses her magic to take on the appearance of an old woman and bribes the ferryman to bring her to the island. There, she adopts the appearance of a beautiful young woman, enticing Set to flirt with her. She tells him she is a widow whose son has been threatened by a stranger who wants to steal from him the cattle left to him by his dead father. Set condemns the injustice and offers to champion her cause, not realizing that the account she is giving directly parallels his unfair treatment of Horus. Isis changes into a kite and mocks him for having condemned himself out of his own mouth, whereupon Set, recognizing her, childishly bursts into tears and hurries to Ra to complain that she is teasing him.

The incident portrays Isis as the trickster-magician. This side to her nature emerges again in a scandalous turn of events in the same story when Horus approaches his mother for help after having suffered a sexual assault from Set. We shall examine the significance of this assault in the chapter on Set. At this point it is only necessary to say that Isis uses her magic to perpetrate a trick that turns around Set's scheme to discredit Horus so that it rebounds upon Set himself.

In the invocation above, the passage from the *Coffin Texts*, spell 828, beginning "She whose head was cut off with a knife," would appear to refer to a later incident recounted in *The Contendings of Horus and Set*, where Horus grows so frustrated by the interference of his mother in his contest with Set that he strikes off her head in a moment of anger. The magic of Isis is too powerful for her to be killed in this way, and to preserve herself, she changes into a headless flint statue until Thoth revives her by giving her the head of a cow, which may be an attempt to explain why Isis is some-times portrayed with a cow's head (and this again links her with Hathor). This disturbing incident deserves closer ex-amination in order to attempt to understand it.

Horus was provoked into attacking his mother because of the manner in which she intervened in the contest. Horus and Set, in the form of hippopotamuses, were com-peting to see who could stay underwater longest. They were both in the river for so long that Isis, fearing that Set was killing Horus, threw a harpoon into the water, intending to strike Set, but accidentally spearing Horus instead. He called out, saying that she had struck her own son, and Isis quickly withdrew the harpoon. She threw it again, this time striking Set; but Set called out, reminding Isis that he was her brother, and, feeling compassion for him, she withdrew the harpoon. From Horus's point of view, his own mother has betrayed both himself and his father by sympathizing with Osiris's murderer, the enemy whom he has been brought up to defeat in order to avenge his father's death. Isis, on the other hand, has divided loyalties: although she deplores Set's murdering of her husband, she also recognizes him as kin, as one who, no less than Osiris, has been her brother since they all shared Nut's womb, together with her twin sister, Nephthys. These relationships are abnormally intimate; Isis may even be feeling a pang of remorse for allowing Set to be the sibling who was unwittingly excluded in the past and whom she has not loved as much as she has loved Osiris and Nephthys, perhaps thereby giving him reason for his jealousy. Isis has a moment of uncertainty, recognizing the complexities of relationships, duties, and moral decisions, and so she relinquishes her attack on Set. Horus, on the other hand, sees the ethics of the situation in black and white: If Isis is siding with his enemy, then she must have become an enemy too, and so he strikes out at her. If it were not for the incomparable magical powers of Isis to transform herself in the nick of time, Horus would surely have killed her. By adopting the form of a statue of flint, Isis not only saves herself but prevents Horus from becoming a murderer, no better than the evil Set.

This strange episode, at first apparently so grotesque and distasteful, can be seen to hold a deeper wisdom when examined more closely. How, indeed, do we oppose evil and seek to defeat it without becoming compromised in the process and resorting to the same monstrous behavior that we deplore in the wrongdoers whom we are opposing? This problem can arise in any situation of conflict, in wars, in matters of dealing with criminals, and in private quarrels where people might seek vengeance. The death penalty for convicted murderers and the use of nerve gas in wars are examples of issues that arouse controversy for this very reason. In the midst of the conflict, Isis takes the form of a headless flint statue, unrecognizable by the other gods, except the ever wise and watchful Thoth: she is resilient, indestructible, undefeated, and enduring; biding her time patiently until the reckless passion is past, and wisdom, in the form of Thoth, comes to her aid.

Horus pays dearly for his loss of self-control and descent into barbarity. The line "She who cleared Horus's vision for him," which appears later in the passage above from spell 828, seems to relate to a subsequent incident in *The Contendings of Horus and Set*, in which Hathor restores the eyes of Horus. In this story, Horus retreats up a mountain with the decapitated stone head of Isis. While Horus is resting on the mountain, Set attacks him and gouges out his eyes. This physical blindness is surely symbolic of the moral blindness that preceded it, specifically, when Horus attacked his own mother. Only the goddess herself, in her aspect as Hathor, the lady of love and beauty, can restore his lost vision: Only love can redeem him once he has descended into Set's darkness. Here, Set and Horus, in a moral sense, have become scarcely indistinguishable, hence Horus's inability to defend himself against his adversary's assault. A further meaning implied here is that one cannot hide away from evil and close one's eyes to it, or rest in one's vigilance against it, for in such circumstances it is possible to be overcome by it and rendered helpless in the face of it.

The line "She who bent Set on account of her utterance," also in the extract from spell 828 above, probably refers to the incident that we described in the chapter on Osiris, in which Set was made to bend down for Osiris to sit upon. The testimony of Isis against him would have been instrumental in bringing this about.

It can be seen from all this that Isis is an unusual combination of mother goddess, funerary goddess, and shapeshifting trickster-magician, which allows her to conform to the conventional feminine stereotypes of devoted wife, loving mother, and mourning widow, while also displaying a more sinister and subversive aspect as a magician of such power that she can overthrow Ra himself and realize her true nature as a manifestation of the Supreme Being. Courageous, loving, loyal, resourceful, clever, pitiful as a victim, stubbornly refusing to accept defeat, Isis is portrayed in the myths as the most psychologically complex of all the Egyptian deities, seemingly as humanly vulnerable as she is supernaturally powerful and indestructible. In the *Coffin Texts*, spell 148, Isis describes herself as "one more spirit-like and august than the gods." In the spell called the Legend of Ra and Isis, we are told: "Her heart was more rebellious than an infinite number of men, more smart than an infinite number of gods. She was more clever than an infinite number of spirits" (Borghouts, 1978, p. 51). In the stories about her, it always seems ambiguous as to whether she is a goddess who has been incarnated in human form or a woman who has made herself and Osiris divine by means of her magic.

This is important for understanding the appeal of the Osirian aspect of Egyptian religion, the reason for the enormous popularity of Isis, and the reason for the successful spread of Isianism over such a wide region. The popularity of Isis was, and still is for her thousands of modern devotees, largely due to her personal qualities, her ability to empathize with human suffering on account of her own tribulations on Earth, and her willingness and power to help those in distress by means of her magic. More than this, however, Isis is the goddess who awakens the Osiris-nature in every follower of the religion. As we saw in the chapter on Osiris, this god can be regarded as the hidden, divine nature of every individual; and the vision of the "sun at midnight"—the recognition of one's true nature as an immortal soul of divine origin incarnated in human form—is the very heart of the Mysteries of Osiris. This means that by applying a mystical interpretation, the invocation above can be seen as a description of the effect that Isis has upon the souls of each of her devotees: as "Mistress of the hidden mysteries," she works her magic on the unaware soul that is initially an "inert one" who has "turned [its] back" on the Divine, and she "spiritualizes" this inert one so that the soul "rejoices when [it] sees her," taking on the role of Osiris in loving Isis, and so realizing its own divine, immortal nature. The sexual metaphor should not be taken literally to imply anything about the gender or sexual orientation of the devotee: Isis is the Divine Spouse in the same sense that Jesus, for Christians, is called the Bridegroom. Isis, like Jesus, is a Savior who redeems the human soul through love; this view of her was very apparent in the Graeco–Roman cult of Isianism.

In the *Hermetica* text, "Kore Kosmu" (Scott, 1993), Isis tells Horus that human beings were originally spirits living in a heavenly realm, but were punished for disobedience to God by being incarnated on Earth, where they forgot their former spiritual state and committed greater sins. She goes on to describe how she and Osiris, who is an "efflux" of God, both incarnated on Earth to educate fallen humanity and institute religious practices, ascending to heaven once their work was done. Similar beliefs, of course, are the basis of Christianity. Isis and Osiris are the human face of God, incarnating on Earth as intercessors between humans and the Divine—the roles later taken on by Mary and Jesus. In *The Golden Ass* (Apuleius), the hero, Lucius, acknowledges that Isis, unlike other Pagan deities, has power even over fate and can divert the stars from harmful courses (according to astrology). It is through her love that he is saved from his wretched condition as an ass, a creature of Set, and he returns that love by becoming her sincere devotee. Isis herself appears to Lucius to explain that she is not only identical with major goddesses worshipped all over the known world, but that she is the single manifestation of all gods as well as goddesses. Here, as in the closing prayer above, there is no doubt about her status as the Supreme Being.

FIFTEEN

SET

Invocation

I call upon you who are in the empty air, you who are terrible, invisible, almighty, a god of gods, you who cause destruction and desolation, you who hate a stable household, you who were driven out of Egypt and have roamed foreign lands, you who shatter everything and are not defeated. I call upon you, Typhon Set . . .

Come to me, you who are in the everlasting air, you who are invisible, almighty, creator of the gods. Come to

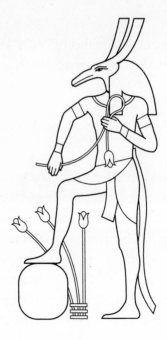

me, you who are the unconquerable daimon. Come to me, you who are never grieved for your own brother, Set....

> —*Papyri Graecae Magicae VII, 940–68; and Papyri Demoticae Magicae xiv, 675–94 (Papyri Graecae Magicae XIVc. 16–27), in* The Greek Magical Papyri in Translation, *edited by Hans Dieter Betz.*

O Set, possessed of your power, Great Longhorn dwelling in the northern sky when the Longhorn is caused to ascend to the northern sky, see, you have come under my feet; give me air among the utnu who give rest to the celestial kine.

> —Coffin Texts, *spell 408, translation by R. O. Faulkner.*

Reply

I am a Man of an infinite number of cubits, whose name is "Evil Day." As for the day of giving birth and becoming pregnant—there is no giving of birth and sycamores will not bear figs.

—*Spell 102 in* Ancient Egyptian Magical Texts, *translation by J. F. Borghouts.*

Set (Sutekh, or Seth according to the Greeks) is the younger son of Nut and Geb and the seventh member of the Heliopolitan Ennead. He is portrayed as a man with the head of an unknown, probably fantastical, animal, with a long, curved snout and erect, square-tipped ears, or as the animal itself, which has a slim body and forked tail. He is also associated with the pig, wild boar, hippopotamus, crocodile, wild ass, and poisonous creatures—specifically, the snake and the scorpion.

He is one of the oldest gods of Egypt, his totem animal appearing on a mace-head of King Scorpion (c. 3150 BC) found at Hierakonopolis. His earliest cult center, from pre–Dynastic times, was at Nubt, meaning "Gold Town," and was known to the Greeks as Ombos. It is north of Luxor on the west bank of the Nile. Near to here, toward the end of Egyptian civilization, the Ptolemies built the temple of Kom Ombos, which is dedicated to Horus the Elder and Sobek (or Suchos), the crocodile god who may be regarded as a form of Set. Set was also worshipped at Per-medjed, the capital of the nineteenth nome of Upper Egypt (modern el-Bahnasa), called Oxyrhynchus by the

Greeks, where the fish Mormyrus Kannume was held sacred. This fish was said to have eaten the penis of Osiris when the god's body was dismembered by Set. The Set-animal was also the totem on the standard of the eleventh nome of Upper Egypt. Set was indeed the tutelary deity of Upper Egypt, as Horus was of Lower Egypt, the land having been divided between them by Geb, according to myth.

In Plutarch's version of the Osirian myth, Set was not born in the normal way, but ripped himself out of his mother's womb prematurely, his first act being indicative of his general nature: impatient and given to violent impulses. Originally he may have been the god of darkness and storms, but he became associated with violence and destruction of all kinds. His natural manifestations are in thunder, wind, rain, and the harsh, dangerous landscape of the red desert that is beyond the fertile, black silt region of the Nile valley. The black land, Kemet (a name also used for the whole country), belonged to Osiris, who reigned as pharaoh. The red land, Deshret (desert), belonged to Set, who took on the role of an outsider, being regarded as the god of foreigners. These chief characteristics are apparent in the first two texts of the invocation above and in Set's reply. Although we have provided this invocation, you must be extremely cautious about invoking Set. Plainly he is not a god whose help should readily be called upon in normal circumstances, and even in a situation when his great strength may be needed to counter a powerful danger, one should be aware of the possible disturbances that his turbulent presence might cause in one's life.

Set was the patron god of the detested Hyksos invaders who ruled Egypt for a century from 1650 BC. Their capital was at Avaris, where Set was worshipped together with his wives, the Semitic goddesses Anat and Astoreth (Astarte). During the Ramesside Period of the New Kingdom when the kings were devotees of Set, he found favor for a while, being regarded as the god of oases as well as the desert, and he came to be seen as the defender of Ra against the serpent Apep (*Book of the Dead*, chapter 39); but this tolerant view of him did not last, and by the Late Period, Set was identified with Apep himself and could at that point virtually be regarded as the Egyptian equivalent of the devil.

No doubt Set's bad reputation stems from his murdering of Osiris. As Osiris became more popular and important as a focus of devotion, as a savior god who offers hope for a blessed afterlife, Set could not avoid being demonized to a corresponding extent. It may be pointed out, however, that Set's role as murderer of his brother is essential in order for Osiris to become the god of resurrection after death. In earlier times, the Egyptians would have been aware of this, for the concept of duality, as we explained before, was essential to their religious beliefs: in all of the realm of creation there is this duality, sometimes giving rise to conflict and sometimes allowing for the balance of complementary principles. Set has an important part to play in this scheme: As the god of darkness, he provides the complement to Horus, the god of the sun, and as god of the desert, he contrasts with Osiris, god of vegetation and fertility. As an ally of Ra against Apep, his dangerous violence becomes a weapon against the greater danger of the chaos serpent. Being of a similar chaotic nature, Set was probably thought to have powers over Apep in a way that a more benign deity may not, much as Sekhmet, as we have seen, could be both the bringer and destroyer of disease.

Set is described as the brother of Horus as well as the brother of Osiris. An attempt to rationalize this apparent inconsistency has given rise to the notion of there being two Horuses: Horus the Elder, called Haroeris, the brother of Osiris and Set, and Horus the Younger, called Harpocrates or Harsiese, the son of Isis and Osiris. The distinction between the two Horuses is often blurred, but we shall address this further in later chapters. All that needs to be mentioned here is that the concept of two Horuses arose from combining two separate myths. The older myth tells of the fight for the throne between Horus and Set, the gods of light and darkness, the north and the south of Egypt. The second myth tells of the murder of Osiris, which developed over centuries to become central to both the specific set of beliefs surrounding kingship and to Egyptian religious concerns of the agricultural cycle and the destiny of the human soul. Thus the myth of the struggle between Horus and Set became the second part of the Osirian myth with Horus now acting as the avenger of his dead father, even though he is sometimes spoken of as the brother of Set rather than his nephew.

Although Set is cast in the role of adversary in both myths, as a member of the Ennead of Heliopolis he is an aspect of the ninefold godhead, a manifestation of Ra-Atum, and just as much divine as any other member of that company, hence the reference to him as a creator god in the second text of the invocation above. His later identification with Apep placed him outside the divine order, in opposition to the whole of Ra-Atum's creation—a development that broke with tradition and led to Set's statues being destroyed and his image being removed from temple walls, while Thoth sometimes took his place in a ritual capacity.

Of course, this shows that the ancient Egyptians struggled with a problem that troubles people of any era, especially those who are religious and who want to believe in the ultimate goodness of Deity and the divine order of creation: is evil part of the divine plan, or is it an unwanted intrusion from an enemy of God? Much of what may seem evil to us, such as disease, injury, pain, and death, is an intrinsic part of the natural world to which the moral language of good and evil would seem not to apply. If anything is to be born, change, or grow, there must also be destruction, death, and decay to allow space for new plants, animals, and people, and some plants and animals in the food chain must die to provide sustenance for others. All this is according to nature, but for those who believe in Deity, such an order of things must surely be seen as part of the divine plan. Some people, seeing that this would make God responsible for much suffering, prefer to believe there is no Deity rather than believe in one who has made animals that prey on one another, harmful viruses and bacteria that cause disease, parasites, and animals with poisonous stings and bites, and who allows natural disasters such as floods, hurricanes, volcanic eruptions, and earthquakes.

We may say that the terms "good" and "evil" cannot apply to natural phenomena and non-sentient animals that have no moral sense and that these terms properly apply only to the actions of sentient beings; but surely the Supreme Being is sentient and therefore subject to being held responsible for what he or she brings about or allows to happen. When we see what goes on in the world and try to imagine the kind of Deity that might be behind it all, it may well seem that such a Being is both beneficent and malevolent. The tendency to want to see God as entirely good, and evil as an enemy force intruding from outside, like the serpent Apep, is counterbalanced by the need to see God as being fully in control of his or her creation or at least more powerful than any opposing force of evil. However, phenomena such as carnivorous animals and earthquakes raise the persistent question of whether Deity might not itself be responsible for at least some of the evils in the world. The troubling fact remains: If Deity exists, either it is too weak to overthrow an evil enemy, or lacks the will to oppose it, or Deity itself causes at least some of the evil.

The ancient Egyptians responded to the problem of evil with two explanations. On the boundaries of Ra's creation is the chaos serpent Apep, the ultimate enemy of everything that exists, whose emissaries, in the form of evil spirits, might occasionally introduce pockets of chaos into the orderly realm of creation. There is also an enemy within, part of the mysterious, ambiguous, unpredictable nature of Deity, and that is Set, the divine darkness, the evil face of God.

Set's murdering of Osiris has already been described in the chapter on Osiris, so we shall examine here his relationship with Horus. There are many references in ancient Egyptian texts to an incident in the struggle between Horus and Set for the throne, in which Horus received an injury to his eye and Set received a corresponding injury to his testicles. The usual interpretation of this is that the two gods had a violent fight in which Set gouged out one of Horus's eyes and Horus retaliated by castrating him.

Some texts refer to Set making sexual advances on Horus. The fullest account of this is in *The Contendings of Horus and Set*, which relates an unsavory and somewhat ridiculous series of events that cannot be described in polite terms. Horus and Set have been presenting their rival claims to kingship before a tribunal of the gods when Set appears to agree to a truce and invites Horus to his house to "have a good time." Later developments indicate that Horus is still only a boy and distinctly naive. He goes home with Set, and when night comes, they lie down in the same bed and Set sexually assaults him. In a passage in the *Petrie Papyri* (Kaster, 1995, p. 256) referring to the same incident, Set first tries to seduce Horus by admiring his buttocks, but Horus threatens to tell his mother and goes to Isis to explain what has happened. Isis instructs him to place his hand between his buttocks when Set attempts intercourse, so as to catch Set's semen in his hand. According to *The Contendings of Horus and Set*, Horus does this instinctively, without prompting from Isis, then shows his mother his hands. With a cry, she cuts off the hands and throws them into the river, replacing them with new hands by means of her magic.

Isis collects some of Horus's semen and spreads it on the lettuce in Set's garden. When Set eats the lettuce, bizarrely he becomes pregnant, and so the two gods return to the tribunal where Set claims to have "done the task of a man" on Horus. The other gods, rather than extending sympathy to Horus, spit and vomit at him in contempt. Consequently, Horus is depicted as the humiliated and degraded loser in the conflict. Horus denies Set's claim and asks that the semen of Set be called forth. Thoth complies with this request and Set's semen answers from the river. Thoth then summons the semen of Horus, which replies from inside the pregnant Set. At Thoth's command, it issues from Set's brow as a golden disc, which Thoth then places on his own head. This unexpected turn of events influences the gods in Horus's favor and the conflict continues along the more conventional lines of a formal contest.

The golden disc to which Set "gives birth" would seem to be the moon, as it is claimed as his own by Thoth, the moon god; but Thoth himself is the personification of the moon, so in this sense Thoth becomes the son of Set and also the son of Horus. The moon is also known as the Eye of Horus (or, as explained earlier, the Wedjat Eye, meaning the "whole eye" or "eye that was healed"). As mentioned in previous chapters, *The Contendings of Horus and Set* describes another incident in the battle in which Set attacks Horus and pulls out both his eyes, which are subsequently restored by Hathor.

All conventional interpretations portray the injuries, to the eye and testicles in this conflict, taking place in the context of a vicious fight, but H. Te Velde, in his book *Seth, God of Confusion*, takes a rather different view. The central thesis of the book is that the two gods are engaged in a homoerotic game that leads to misunderstanding and conflict. Set, he says, as the "god of confusion," has an irregular sexuality that does not recognize the normal boundaries of heterosexuality and homosexuality. His unusual proclivities drive him to assault Horus, rape his wife Anat when she is dressed as a man, and make sexual advances toward Isis, which include imprisoning her in a spinning-house, as described in the previous chapter. According to Te Velde, the damage to Horus's eye is not deliberate blinding, but represents a draining of vital power when he is subjected to the sexual advances of Set, and correspondingly, the damage to Set's testicles is not castration, but represents the loss of virile energy when Set's semen is spilled in his failing to achieve union with Horus.

The idea that Horus and Set might be involved in a stormy homosexual relationship, as Te Velde argues, seems odd, but it could help to explain the ambivalent attitude the two gods have for one another, sometimes on friendly terms, sometimes fighting frantically. If they had inflicted such horrendous injuries on one another, would reconciliation really be possible? Yet the feud ends, and they are both "satisfied" through the healing intervention of Thoth, their strangely-conceived son.

Set's official wife appears to be his sister Nephthys, but his relationship with her is less than satisfactory. It may be that the god Anubis is Set's son by Nephthys, but on the other hand, as we shall see in the next chapter, the father of Anubis may be Osiris. As mentioned in the chapter on Neith, Set's other two wives were given to him as compensation for losing sovereignty over Egypt.

As we have seen in previous chapters, when Set is finally defeated and revealed as a liar, a murderer, and a usurper of the throne, he is made to bend down so that Osiris may sit upon him. Various texts in the funerary literature refer to his carrying Osiris on his back, and also helping Osiris lead the deceased up to heaven by means of a ladder. The text used for the invocation above is a prayer to Set to provide air for the soul traveling in the spirit realm among the utnu. It is not known exactly what these utnu were. Here Set is the Great Longhorn in the northern sky, a designation that identifies him with the constellation of the Great Bear. He is also a sky god in his roles as god of thunder and rain, and protector in the bark of Ra.

On a personal level for the individual devotee, Set may be regarded as an individual's lower nature. The ancient

Egyptian funerary texts frequently make reference to the defeat of enemies, yet the virtuous religious person who aspires to enter the blessed realm of Osiris would have few, if any, enemies in the literal sense of fellow human beings. These "enemies" are surely of a spiritual nature, in the form of the many temptations and vices that might corrupt a person who does not guard against them. Viewed in this context, Set and his band of seventy-two conspirators who trap Osiris in the chest or mummy case can be seen as the ensnaring vices that might keep a person enveloped in a materialistic view of the world, which leads to obsession with fulfilling the desires of the body and seeking wealth, power, and physical gratification. On the other hand, Osiris, as we have seen, represents the true, spiritual self of the individual that is one with God. The sensually-indulgent lower nature might prefer to deny the higher self altogether, to shut out any awareness of it, all the better to indulge material desires and cravings, even if this leads to spiritual death.

The lower nature can never be entirely suppressed, of course, as a human being has physical needs, but in its proper role in the spiritually developed person, it is commuted to the service of the higher self, as passions are turned to a spiritual end and a desire develops to help others as well as oneself. The myths and sacred texts present Set as foolish, impulsive, childish—a braggart and a bully who seeks instant gratification; but he is also strong, daring, sensuous, passionate, and charming, and it is apparent that the positive aspects of his nature can be utilized in a supportive, helpful, and strengthening manner. Te Velde (1977, p. 52) argues that the intervention of Isis, to prevent Set's penetration of Horus and to bring about Horus's impregnation of Set instead is a way of making the darkness subordinate to the light, so that the light suffuses the darkness rather than being consumed by it. The higher self, now represented by Horus as the reborn Osiris, is essentially divine and redeems the lower nature represented by Set. In other words, light emerges from the darkness as the golden Eye of Horus on the brow of Set, the moon in the dark face of the night sky. Thus, the two warring gods are reconciled, and the moon, the Wedjat Eye, becomes a symbol of hope and salvation, of harmony, wisdom, and justice—all the qualities represented by the moon god Thoth. In the Egyptian dualistic scheme of things, darkness is a brother to the light, and even the most basic animal drives and impulses of the lower nature can be turned to a good end in aiding the development of the spiritually maturing individual.

SIXTEEN

NEPHTHYS

Invocation

I have come to you, O Nephthys
   I have come to you, Sun Bark of night;
I have come to you, You who are Just in the Reddening;
   I have come to you, Stars of the Northern Sky—
      remember me.

Gone is Orion, caught by the underworld,
   yet cleansed and alive in the Beyond;
Gone is Sothis, caught by the underworld,
   yet cleansed and alive in the Beyond.
Gone am I, caught by the underworld,
   yet cleansed and alive in the Beyond.

It is well with me, with them,

   it is quiet for me, for them,

Within the arms of my father,

   within the arms of Atum.

—Pyramid Texts, *utterance 216, translation by John L. Foster, in*
Hymns, Prayers, and Songs: an Anthology of Ancient Egyptian
Lyric Poetry, *pp. 30–1.*

Nephthys is a Greek name. The Egyptian name of Nephthys is Nebet-Het, meaning "lady of the house" or "lady of
the temple." She is the younger daughter of Nut and Geb,
the twin sister of Isis, and wife of Set. Although an important goddess by reason of her being a member of the He-

liopolitan Ennead, Nephthys is also strangely obscure, seeming to have few characteristics in her own right, her nature determined chiefly by her relationships with other deities, especially Isis. The Greeks regarded her as a form of Aphrodite, ancient spells show her in a healing role, and she has been called the goddess of hidden things. Modern commentators have seen her as a goddess of nature, of the moon, of the home (a housewife), and of death and decay. This rather confusing and contradictory image of her has sometimes given rise to the impression that she herself is shadowy, confusing and possibly unreliable. It is more accurate to say that information about her has been sparse.

Nephthys is usually portrayed as a woman with the hieroglyphs of her name—a basket and a house—on her head. When she is paired with Isis, the two sisters are shown as identical in dress and appearance, with or without wings, distinguished only by the hieroglyphs on their heads or in accompanying inscriptions. Both may also take the form of serpents or kites.

Nephthys is seen primarily as a goddess of death and mourning who comforts the bereaved. From the time of the *Pyramid Texts*, she is represented in the myths as the companion of the mourning Isis, helping her to find the body of Osiris that is drifting in the Nile. She and Isis are depicted guarding the mummified body, Nephthys usually at the head and Isis at the foot. In the same capacity as guardian of the dead, Nephthys is the subject of one of the

golden goddess statues surrounding the shrine of Tutankhamun, the others being Isis, Neith, and Serket.

The text used for the invocation above is probably most
suitable to use as a prayer in a situation of dying and be-
reavement. In this text, Nephthys appears as the guide and
comforter of the dead. The stars of the northern sky, mentioned here, were believed by the Egyptians to be a desir-
able destination for the souls of the dead. As the goddess
who presides over the transition from life to death, Nephthys was associated with the unpleasant physical aspects of
death as well; specifically, with the process of a corpse de-
caying (which was to be prevented by mummification) and
with the mummy-wrapping bandages. The bandages are
identified with the tresses of Nephthys in the *Pyramid Texts*,
utterance 553.

Nephthys is also described in the above invocation as
the goddess of the evening sun, the Sekhtet boat or Night
Bark, as it is sometimes called, complementing Isis as the
goddess of the dawn and the Atet boat or Day Bark.

Nephthys was not only associated with the transition
from day to night and from life to death, but also with the
boundary region between the fertile land of Osiris and the
desert land of Set, and this perhaps suggests a partnership
with both gods. In a later tradition, Nephthys becomes
tragically instrumental in the events leading to the death of
Osiris. According to Plutarch ("Isis and Osiris"), Isis realized
that Nephthys had made love to Osiris when she saw a gar-
land of melilot flowers that Osiris had given to Nephthys.

Osiris was not responsible for the adultery, as Nephthys, the identical twin of Isis, had been able to pass herself off as Isis, and Osiris had simply assumed that the woman in his bed was his wife. Isis also discovers that, as a result of this union, Nephthys gave birth to a son, Anubis, but had immediately exposed the child to kill him, so that her husband Set would not find out, hoping thus to avoid his jealous rage. Isis rescues the child, to whom she has been led by dogs.

A spell in the *Greek Magical Papyri*, (Betz, 1996, IV: 94–153), describes how Thoth comes across his "daughter" Isis in a dirty and disheveled state after she has been wandering on the mountain weeping because she has learned of the adulterous union between Nephthys and Osiris. E. A. Wallis Budge (1973, 1:14) cites a fourth-century Christian writer, Julius Firmicus Maternus, who gives a rather garbled account of the Osirian myth in which Isis is married to Set. Maternus says Set murders Osiris out of jealousy when he finds that Isis has been having an affair with Osiris. The discovery that his wife has been having an affair with Osiris may well be Set's motive for the murder, but the unfaithful wife is surely Nephthys, and not Isis, the very model of matrimonial fidelity who is married to Osiris.

The lady of love and death is a familiar figure in the myth and folklore of other cultures: the Sumerian goddess Inanna banishes her lover Dumuzi to the underworld; the Phrygian god Attis castrates himself and bleeds to death when his love for Cybele is unrequited; Artemis kills Orion with an arrow after he makes sexual advances to her; and in the Bible, Delilah lures Samson to his downfall, while Eve's seduction of Adam into eating the forbidden fruit condemns the whole human race to mortality. At first sight, such a femme fatale is absent from the myth of Isis and Osiris with its central theme of true love that triumphs over death, but a closer look reveals her presence in the mysterious figure of Nephthys. The unloved wife, the devious secret lover, the frightened mother who abandons her child, a lady whose best achievement is the mourning of her dead brother, Nephthys is a strange antiheroine of a goddess. In all these respects she seems to be the dark or negative counterpart of Isis, but unlike Set, who has a similar function in relation to Osiris and Horus, Nephthys is never portrayed as evil. Her qualities are complementary to those of Isis rather than directly opposed, and her weaknesses are very much a part of her appeal. Like Isis, she knows all too well from personal experience the frailties of the human condition, but where Isis heroically triumphs over adversity, Nephthys is more often a victim to it.

Nephthys appears very oddly in a spell in the *Greek Magical Papyri* (Betz, 1996, XIa, 1–40) that is intended to conjure up the old serving-woman of Apollonius of Tyana, a famous magician. The instructions stipulate that one should use the blood of a black dog to mark an ass's skull with certain magical symbols, then place the skull under the left foot while standing at a crossroads, and invoke the goddess called Mistress of the House, which is a translation of Nephthys's name. The ass, as mentioned in the previous chapter, is sacred to Set, while the black dog would seem to relate to Anubis. The location of the crossroads suggests some association of Nephthys with the Greek goddess of the moon and magic, Hekate, to whom crossroads are sacred. When invoked, Nephthys first appears as a beautiful young woman, but upon being told by the magician that she is required for domestic service, she changes to an old servant. The goddess then leaves the old woman, who becomes a separate entity from herself, but binds her to the magician's service by giving one of the woman's molars and an ass's tooth to the magician for him to wear.

The figure of Nephthys has become remarkably debased in this spell. The occurrence of the Egyptian word *het* or *hwt*, meaning "temple" or "house," as a component of her name was certainly not originally intended to mean that she was simply a housewife or housekeeper. Most significantly, there was a town called Hwt or Hiw (Diospolis Parva) in the seventh nome of Upper Egypt, where Nephthys had a temple called the Mansion of the Sistrum, so her name probably derives from this main cult center.

An important role of Nephthys is to help women in childbirth and with the nursing of children. In a story called "King Cheops and the Magicians" in the *Westcar Papyrus* (Kaster, 1995), she, along with Isis, Meskhenet, the goddess of childbirth, and Heket, a fertility goddess also associated with childbirth, assists at the birth of some divinely begotten triplets who are destined to be kings of

Egypt. In the myths about Isis and Horus, Nephthys helps Isis by nursing Horus when he is a baby.

So Nephthys has a number of aspects to her character, but most of all it seems that she is a caring and helpful goddess, a midwife, a healer, a child minder, a nurse to the sick and dying, a caretaker for the dead, and a comforter to the bereaved. Women have traditionally occupied these roles down the centuries, often enjoying little credit for what they do as their service is taken for granted; and perhaps it is for the same reason that Nephthys has always seemed to be hidden in the shadow of her more spectacularly heroic sister, Isis.

SEVENTEEN

HORUS THE ELDER

Invocation

The doors of the sky are opened,
The doors of the firmament are thrown open at dawn
    for Horus of the Gods.
He goes up into the Field of Rushes,
He bathes in the Field of Rushes.
The doors of the sky are opened,
The doors of the firmament are thrown open at dawn
    for Harakhti.
He goes up into the Field of Rushes,
He bathes in the Field of Rushes.

The doors of the sky are opened,
The doors of the firmament are thrown open at dawn
    for Horus of the East.
He goes up into the Field of Rushes,
He bathes in the Field of Rushes.
The doors of the sky are opened,
The doors of the firmament are thrown open at dawn
    for Horus of Shezmet.
He goes up into the Field of Rushes,
He bathes in the Field of Rushes.

—Pyramid Texts, *utterance 325, translation by R. O. Faulkner,*
   reprinted by permission of Oxford University Press.

May you wake in peace, O Purified, in peace!
May you wake in peace, O Horus of the East, in peace!
May you wake in peace, O Soul of the East, in peace!
May you wake in peace, O Harakhti, in peace!
May you sleep in the Night-bark,
May you wake in the Day-bark,
For you are he who oversees the gods,
There is no god who oversees you!

> —Pyramid Texts, *utterance 573, translation by R. O. Faulkner,*
> *reprinted by permission of Oxford University Press.*

Closing

Enter in peace, leave in peace, go in happiness. For life is in His hand, peace is in His grasp, all good things are with Him. There is food for him who remains at His table, and nourishment for him who partakes of His offerings. No misfortune or evil will befall the one who lives on His beneficence, neither is there damnation for the one who serves Him for His care reaches to heaven and His security to earth and His protection is greater than that of all the gods.

> —*From the Temple of Horus at Edfu, in* The House of Horus at
> Edfu, *by Barbara Watterson, p. 80.*

The Egyptians had more than one concept of Horus; they also had other falcon gods, some of whom became assimilated to Horus. Because of this, he can seem a confusing god. The ancient Egyptians themselves did not always make a clear distinction between the various Horus gods, so it may be best to regard him as one god with many aspects.

However, to try to provide some clarity, we present here the information about the two main forms of Horus in two chapters, leaving Horus the Younger, the son of Isis, for the next chapter.

Horus the Elder (Heru-ur to the Egyptians and Haroeris to the Greeks) was the oldest state god, identifiable by name from the Early Dynastic Period (c. 3100 BC), although the unnamed falcon that appears on the palette of an earlier king, Narmer (3050 BC), is probably Horus. As we have seen, the king himself was regarded as a manifestation of Horus on Earth. In the chapter on Geb, we mentioned that in the *Turin Royal Canon*, a papyrus from the Nineteenth Dynasty that lists the kings of Egypt, Horus was believed to be one of the gods who governed on Earth in the golden age of the First Time; his reign was followed by that of the goddess Maat, after which came the reigns of kings known as the Shemsu Hor, the Followers of Horus, who were semidivine. All later kings were emulating these first rulers, and as Horus, each of them strove to reestablish in Egypt the Zep Tepi, the First Time, as a condition of order and justice as close to perfection as possible.

Horus the Elder was thought to be either the son of Hathor and Ra or, in later times, of Nut and Geb. Hathor is also regarded as the wife of Horus. He is portrayed as a falcon or a man with a falcon's head. As the brother of Set, he is the tutelary god of Lower Egypt while Set is the god of Upper Egypt. The Egyptian name for Horus is Heru, Hor, or Har, which means "face" or "distant." It resembles the

Egyptian word *horet*, meaning "sky." Horus personifies the distant face of the sky whose eyes are the sun and the moon. Horus is the face of the sky by day, while Set is the face of the sky by night. However, a form of Horus called Hor-Khenty-en-Irty, meaning "Horus foremost one without eyes," is the sky in which neither sun nor moon is visible.

During the Old Kingdom, Horus was regarded as the god of the east, associated with the sunrise, which is very apparent in the *Pyramid Texts* extract in the invocation above. A name used for Horus here is Harakhti (Heru-khuti), meaning "Horus of the horizon," and the Field of Rushes also mentioned is a region of the sky. Another form of Horus is Hor-em-Akhet (Harmachis in Greek), which means "Horus in the horizon," but refers to the leonine image of the god as the Sphinx, so although these names seem similar, they have different connotations and should not be confused. Originally a god of the sky, Horus, as we can see in the above invocation, came to be regarded as a solar deity, and at Heliopolis, where he became incorporated into the Osirian myth as Harsiesis, the son of Isis and Osiris, he was also assimilated to Ra as Ra-Harakhti.

As Horus of Behdet, a town in the delta region, Horus the Elder was worshipped as a warrior god in the form of a winged disc and a hawk-headed man. He had a sanctuary in Letopolis (called Khem by the Egyptians, now Kom Ausim) in the western delta, where he was Horus Khenty-Irty. He was also closely associated with Nekhen (now Kom el-Ahmar), called by the Greeks Hierakonpolis, meaning "town of the hawk." This was an important settlement in the pre–Dynastic Era where Horus the Elder was assimilated to an earlier hawk god, Nekheny. Edfu (Mesen) was a cult center of Horus from at least the Pyramid Age; it became his most important center of worship from the time of the New Kingdom. In his later temple there, built by the Ptolemies, he was venerated together with his consort, Hathor, and their son, Harsomtus (Har-mau, "Horus the uniter") who is another form of Horus, identified with the king as sustainer of the peaceful union of the Two Lands of Egypt. At Edfu, Horus the Younger was also worshipped.

EIGHTEEN

HARSIESIS

Invocation

Thy father Atum hath woven for thee a beautiful chaplet of victory to be placed on thy living brow, O thou who lovest the gods, and thou shalt live for ever. Osiris-khent-Amentet hath made thee to triumph over thine enemies, and thy father Geb hath decreed for thee all his inheritance. Come, therefore, O Horus, son of Isis, for thou, O son of Osiris, sittest upon the throne of thy father Ra to overthrow thine enemies, for he hath ordained for thee the two lands to their utmost limits. Atum hath also ordained this, and the company of the gods hath confirmed the splendid power of

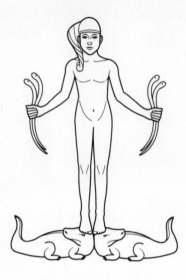

the victory of Horus the son of Isis and the son of Osiris
for ever and for ever.

—Book of the Dead, *chapter 19, translation by E. A. Wallis Budge.*

Reply

I am Horus, the Falcon who is on the battlements of the
Mansion of Him whose name is hidden. My flight aloft has
reached the horizon, I have overpassed the gods of the sky,
I have made my position more prominent than that of the
Primeval Ones. The Contender has not attained my first
flight, my place is far from Set, the enemy of my father
Osiris. I have used the roads of eternity to the dawn, I go
up in my flight, and there is no god who can do what I have
done. . . . I am Horus, born of Isis, whose protection was

made within the egg; the fiery blast of your mouths does not attack me, and what you may say against me does not reach me, I am Horus, more distant of place than men or gods; I am Horus, son of Isis.

I indeed am Horus within the egg, one acute of vision, who is on his belly in the nest. . . . I have displayed my power, I mount up to the horizon, I am supported on Geb, I travel on the sunshine. . . . I hear what my mother Isis says to me, for I am the child of Ra, the companion of Ra, I am the marvelous one who is in the gate of eternity, my allotted term is everlastingness, and I come to you at will.

—Coffin Texts, *spells 148 and 150, translation by R. O. Faulkner.*

Horus the Younger is the son of Isis, known to Egptians as Hor-sa-Aset, and known to Greeks as Harsiese or Harsiesis. As explained previously, he was conceived by magical means after the death of his father Osiris and brought up in secret by Isis. He is also called Horus the Child (Hor-pa-khred in Egyptian, or Harpocrates in Greek) and Horus-avenger-of-his-father (Hor-nedj-her-itef in Egyptian or Harendotes in Greek). As a child, he is depicted as a young naked boy wearing his hair in the plaited side-lock of youth and often holding one finger to his lips. On the plaques called *cippi*, which bear healing spells and became popular between the eighth century BC and the fourth century AD, he is shown standing on the backs of crocodiles and clutching snakes—signs that he overpowers these dangerous creatures. As an adult, he has the head of a falcon.

We have already mentioned how Isis healed her son of various afflictions, of scorpion stings, and the bites of snakes. She also healed him of burns on more than one occasion, as described in ancient Egyptian spells. The relationship between Isis and Horus is unusually close, but this also has a darker side. In one spell (Borghouts, 1978, p. 88), Isis stands in a river, weeping, after Horus has had intercourse with her, and Horus beheads his mother in a bout of rage as we have seen in *The Contendings of Horus and Set*.

In the first text chosen for the invocation above, Horus is called the son of Osiris, but Atum, Geb, and Ra are referred to as his fathers. This could be because the term "father" is being used in a loose sense of "male ancestor," or it may indicate, as we have seen before, that within the Ennead, the deities of each generation may be regarded as emanations of earlier generations and ultimately as various forms of Ra-Atum. The second text in the invocation also presents Horus the Younger in terms that usually apply to Horus the Elder, as a falcon who flies to the edge of the world, the eastern horizon, at dawn. He is said here to be greater than the "gods of the sky," which are the stars. He has been protected by Atum "within the egg," meaning that Atum provided protection from Set for Isis and her unborn child. Atum does this because the child was the son of Osiris and the rightful heir to the throne. Again, we confront the issue of the Egyptians using the same word for "egg" and "embryo." In this case, the double-meaning word can define Horus in his mother's womb, or, at the same time, allude to a creation myth about Horus the Elder as a falcon emerging from an egg laid at the beginning of the world by the Primeval Goose (Clark, 1978 [1959], pp. 55, 213, and 279, note 76).

For the ancient Egyptians, Horus's status as the heir of Osiris was of great importance in establishing the legitimacy of each new king. The dead king's heir, taking the role of Horus, would perform the Opening of the Mouth ceremony on the king's mummy during the funeral rites. In taking this care to ensure by ritual that the previous king would enjoy a blessed afterlife as Osiris, the heir was able to establish his own position as the future Horus king by acting as the loyal son, even if he were not actually the deceased king's son, as was sometimes the case. The version of the Osirian myth in which Isis resurrects Osiris is a later development, for older texts emphasize the actions of Horus in raising up his father and establishing him as the king in the afterlife.

An important component of Horus's act of restoring Osiris to life is the offering of the Eye of Horus, which, as we have seen, is the "whole" (full) moon. It is appropriate that Horus, the young sun god, should restore to life his dead father, the moon god Osiris, by granting him a portion of his own power and light. The murder and dismemberment of Osiris by Set can (like the injuring of the Eye of Horus) be seen as relating to the waning of the moon. Likewise, the restoration of the Eye of Horus and the restoration of Osiris's body can be equated. The Eye of Horus thus comes to represent healing and wholeness in any context and the establishment of the rightful order. The act of offering the

Wedjat Eye became an important part of the Opening of the Mouth ceremony performed on the mummy of a pharaoh during a funerary rite. During this ceremony, food, clothing, and ritual regalia would be presented to the mummy of the dead king, each item symbolically designated as the Eye of Horus, which has been made by Thoth "whole" or "sound" (as a full moon) after having been previously (when the moon waned) made weak by Set.

There is a sense in which Horus the Younger is a reincarnation of his father, Osiris: his whole motivation seems to be to avenge his father's death and claim the throne for himself. Even his struggles with illness as a child can be interpreted as part of his battle against Set, who is the god presiding over such dangerous animals as the snakes and scorpions that afflict him. If Horus is a reincarnation of Osiris, then the texts alluding to a sexual relationship between him and his mother, Isis, do not seem so shocking. Indeed, Alison Roberts, in her book, *My Heart, My Mother* (2000, p. 126), argues that such an incestuous union is necessary if the fertile forces that ensure regeneration and continuation of new cycles of life are to be passed on from each pharaoh to his successor and if the dead are to continue to receive sustenance in the afterlife. In this capacity, Horus is identified with Min, whom we shall look at in a later chapter.

Horus the Younger, the son of Isis, is very much a figure who represents youth, rebirth, and rejuvenation; he can also be seen as standing for the conscious self that "rules" the whole person. He is the young sun god, the sun of the morning, complementing Osiris as the hidden sun, the sun at midnight. He is also the sun god who is born just after the winter solstice when the days begin to grow longer after the shortest day.

As we have seen, Osiris may be regarded as a hidden, spiritual aspect of oneself that is united to Deity, while Set may be seen as the lower self of uncontrolled drives and impulses. The actions of Horus are very much determined by his relationship with these two gods, just as one's conscious self must relate to the hidden and unconscious parts of oneself. When Horus is a child, he is taught by Isis to beware of Set and to take the throne from him, just as most children are taught by those who bring them up to control themselves—resist impulses that are destructive, thoughtless, and hurtful to others. As we have seen, Set can never be destroyed. He can only be mastered, placed in a subordinate position, and persuaded to cooperate with the forces of light and order. Horus seems to be rather a difficult child, prone to sickness, often in trouble, and constantly appealing to his mother for help; as an adolescent, his relationship with Isis certainly takes a turn for the worse. Metaphorically, these events could be construed as phases in moral and spiritual development. The mature Horus takes control of the situation and overthrows Set, not just by means of his own willpower, but with the intelligent assistance of Isis and Thoth. He then makes peace with Set and establishes Osiris in his heavenly kingdom before ascending the Earthly throne himself. All this can be taken as a metaphor for the process of emotional, moral, and spiritual maturing that is necessary for someone to become a well-balanced person of integrity. So Horus, the weak child and willful adolescent, eventually matures to become like his heavenly father, the wise, gentle, and virtuous Osiris. This is surely a pattern that an initiate of the Osirian mysteries was supposed to follow and is still appropriate for followers of this spiritual path today.

NINETEEN

ANUBIS

Invocation

Hail Anubis! Come to me! O high one, O mighty one, O master of secrets for those in the Underworld, O Pharaoh of those in Amenti, O Chief Physician, O good son of Osiris, he whose face is strong among the gods, you should appear in the Underworld before the hand of Osiris. You should serve the souls of Abydos in order that they all live through you, these souls, the ones of the sacred Underworld. Come to the earth! Reveal yourself to me here today!

—*Papyri Demoticae Magicae, xiv, 1–92, column II, 17, translation by Janet H. Johnson, in* The Greek Magical Papyri in Translation, Volume I, *edited by Hans Dieter Betz.*

Reply

The scepter of him who is in the place of embalming appears, the Wardens of the Chambers are glad, the Great Ones have received their leopard-skins, the staffs stand before the Great Place, for it is Anubis who comes in peace, having appeared as Vizier. He says: Guard yourselves, you whose faces are aken, who see the Pure Place, who come in the following of the Evil One; who enter into the choice places, who create their breaths for him, who prepare the offerings for this great god, the Lord of the gods, who awaken the nau-snakes because of their lords. Go, hold fast within the castle the great [thing] within the setjet, on account of this god who is in the Presence, that he may make fear within his castle—so says Anubis. . . . Seize the Evil

One who is in darkness, execute sentence upon his confed-
erates, and the heart of Him who presides over the Sacred
Booth will be glad when he sees the rejoicing in the Great
Place by Isis, Lady of the Deserts.

—Coffin Texts, *spell 49, translation by R. O. Faulkner.*

Anubis (called Anpu by the Egyptians) is usually regarded
as the son of Nephthys, either by Osiris or Set. Alternative
traditions record that his mother is Hesat, a cow goddess,
or Bast, and that his father is Ra (Hart, 1986). He is portrayed as a jackal or a man with the head of a jackal. A
jackal is a doglike desert animal that scavenges for food,
and can sometimes dig up dead bodies buried in shallow
graves. Because of a jackal's habits, the ancient Egyptians associated it with the dead, but following their usual principle
of placating potentially harmful forces with the aim of di-
verting their energies toward beneficial ends, they conceived
of the jackal god Anubis as a kindly and helpful deity who
embalmed bodies, guided the souls of the dead into the afterlife, and guarded their tombs. Anubis is sometimes called
Neb-ta-djeser, meaning "Lord of the Sacred Land," which
refers to the desert. He is also said to be Tepy-dju-ef, meaning "upon his mountain," which refers to the cliffs overlook-
ing cemeteries in the desert. The black fur of Anubis is not
necessarily the true coloring of jackals and other desert
dogs, but, as in the case of the black skin of Osiris, symbolizes fertility and rebirth by its association with the dark
color of the fertile soil of the Nile valley.

As we have seen in the chapter on Nephthys, there is a strand of Osirian myth, recounted by Plutarch, in which Nephthys abandons Anubis as a baby in order to conceal from her husband Set that she has had a son by Osiris. Isis recovers the baby after being led to it by wild dogs. The implication is that Anubis is a feral child, brought up by animals, and that this is why he has the nature of a jackal. Isis subsequently adopts Anubis as her own son, presumably because she recognizes that his father is her husband. He may be seen as the elder half-brother of Harsieses, or, if Set is his father, the half-brother of Thoth, who may also be a son of Set.

Although he may be Osiris's first-born son, Anubis makes no claim for the throne, being illegitimate. Nevertheless, it makes sense to see him as a complementary god to Horus. He helps Isis and Nephthys to gather the dismembered parts of Osiris's body, and embalms the body to make the first mummy. Together with Horus, Anubis has a prominent role in the Opening of the Mouth ceremony which enables Osiris (or any dead person) to function in the afterlife.

Priests of Anubis would dress as the god, wearing a jackal mask, while performing the rites of mummification and the Opening of the Mouth. This is known from pictures of priests wearing such masks; amazingly, examples of the masks themselves have survived. As the god of embalming, Anubis is called Khenty-seh-netjer, meaning "he who presides over the Sacred Booth." The booth or pavilion, also called the Pure Place, as in the reply above, was a kind of tent in which the embalming took place, although the term might also apply to a sarcophagus. Another epithet of Anubis is Imy-ut, "he who is in the place of embalming." He is sometimes depicted as a jackal lying on top of a chest, which might represent the embalming booth or a box containing the viscera, which were removed from a body before embalming.

In contrast to Horus's brightness, Anubis is a god of the dark, but his darkness, unlike that of Set, is benign. As is clear from the invocation above, he is, like Osiris, a god of the underworld, amenti; but unlike Osiris he has no solar qualities. While Horus is concerned with fighting for justice, avenging his father's murder, and taking his place on Earth as the heir to his throne, Anubis occupies himself with caring for Osiris's dead body and assisting him at his court in the afterlife. Anubis leads the souls of the dead into the judgment hall of Osiris and weighs their hearts on the scales of Maat, the result being entered into the records by Thoth. Anubis is very much a friend to the dead and a helper of the other gods. The text used for his reply above also shows that in his role as a guardian he is uncompromisingly fierce toward evil entities that might threaten anyone under his protection. Unfortunately, this text has become garbled and the definitions of some words (*aken*, *nau*, *setjet*) are not known.

Spells in the *Greek Magical Papyri* (Betz, 1996), such as the one from which the invocation above was taken, show that Anubis came to be seen as a god who is helpful in divination. Perhaps, like his mother Nephthys, he was regarded as a revealer of hidden things. To invoke Anubis, Egyptians were known to spread oil on the surface of water in a bowl and use it as a magic mirror for scrying by lamplight, often using a young boy as a medium. The magician would invoke Anubis and instruct the boy to look into the bowl in which the god's image would appear when he arrived. Anubis might not answer questions himself, but would bring other spirits who would.

In Graeco–Roman culture, Anubis took on a broader role than a god of embalming and guide of the dead; he is also featured in the cult of Isis. Modern practitioners of ancient Egyptian religion often regard him as a guardian and guide in many contexts, not just for the dead.

TWENTY

MIN

Invocation

> I worship Min, I extol arm-raising Horus:
> Hail to you, Min in his procession!
> Tall-plumed, son of Osiris,
> Born of divine Isis.
> Great in Senut, mighty in Ipu,
> You of Coptos, Horus strong-armed,
> Lord of awe who silences pride,
> Sovereign of all the gods!

Fragrance laden when he comes from Medja-land,
Awe inspiring in Nubia,
You of Utent, hail and praise!

—In Ancient Egyptian Literature, *Volume I, by Miriam Lichtheim,*
    p. 204.

Min (called Menu by the Egyptians) is a god of fertility and
procreation, portrayed as an ithyphallic man, his arm
raised, holding a flail and wearing a plumed crown similar
to that worn by Amun. He is a very ancient deity, worshipped from the Early Dynastic Period or earlier, and is
featured in temples all over Egypt, but his main cult centers
were in Upper Egypt at Coptos (Gebtu, to the ancient

Egyptians, and now called Qift) and Ipu or Khent-Min (called Khemmis or Panopolis by the Greeks, who identified Min with their god Pan). He was regarded as the protector of the caravans that set off from these towns to the mining regions of the eastern desert. The bull and the lettuce are sacred to him.

Min is primarily an agricultural and fertility god who provides healthy crops and plentiful harvests. By the time of the Middle Kingdom, he came to be identified with Horus, the son of Isis, as can be seen from the invocation above. Sometimes he was regarded as the consort of Isis, with Horus as their child. Like Osiris, he can be depicted in the form of a mummy or with black flesh, symbolizing the regenerative power of the earth that emanates from the underworld or the realm of the dead in continuous cycles of new life.

TWENTY-ONE

KHONSU

Invocation

Hail to you, Khonsu in Thebes Nefer-hotep, the noble child
who came forth from the lotus, Horus, lord of time, he is one.
. . . O silver, lord of silver, O circuit of the underworld, lord of
the circuit of the underworld, lord of the disk, the great god,
the vigorous bull, the Son of the Ethiopian, come to me.

> —*Papyri Demoticae Magicae, xiv, 239–95, translation by Janet H.*
> *Johnson, in* The Greek Magical Papyri in Translation, *Volume I,*
> *edited by Hans Dieter Betz.*

Khons, or Khonsu, is a moon god. He is the son of Amun
and Mut, and with them he formed a divine triad at
Thebes. In Amun's temple at Karnak, Khonsu had his own

precinct. He is usually portrayed as a child wearing the side-lock of youth and a lunar headdress, but sometimes he has the head of a falcon, which may account for his identification with Horus in the invocation above. As Khonsu-pa-khered, "Khonsu the child," he resembles Hor-pa-khered, or Harpocrates, the child form of Horus.

The name Khonsu means "wanderer," referring to the movement of the moon in the sky. He was known as Heseb Ahau, "reckoner of the life-span," relating to the moon's phases being used to count the passage of time in months. In the invocation above, he is called "lord of time," thus it seems that his help may be sought when attempting to predict future events.

TWENTY-TWO

IMHOTEP

Invocation

Hail to you, kind-hearted god,
Imhotep son of Ptah!
Come to your house ...
May its people see you with joy!
Receive what is presented there,
Inhale the incense,
Refresh your body with libation!

... Men applaud you,
Women worship you,
One and all exalt your kindness!

For you heal them,
You revive them,
You renew your father's creation. . . .

—*From the Temple of Ptah at Karnak, in* Ancient Egyptian Literature, *Volume III, by Miriam Lichtheim, pp. 105–6.*

Imhotep, called Imouthes by the Greeks, is highly unusual
among Egyptian deities as he was a real man whose achieve-
ments in life were so impressive that he became deified after
his death, which was not a normal Egyptian practice. He
was the vizier of the Third Dynasty pharaoh, King Djoser,
and is believed to be the designer of the king's Step Pyramid at Saqqara. The Egyptian priest, Manetho (third century BC), who wrote a history of Egypt in Greek, says that
Imhotep invented the technique of building with cut stone.

As a sculptor and architect, he came to be seen as the son of the sculptor god Ptah, by a human mother, Khreduankh.

Imhotep was also highly regarded as a scribe, having composed a book of instruction for living wisely, although this has now been lost. There was a genre of such works in Egypt, often called "precepts," which are similar to the books of Proverbs and Ecclesiastes in the Bible.

In particular, Imhotep was venerated as a healer, as can be seen in the invocation above, where his healing miracles are praised for being a renewal of the act of creation by his "father," the god Ptah. In his healing capacity, Imhotep was identified by the Greeks with their god Aesculapius or Asclepius. In the Ptolemaic Period, the cult of Imhotep found a place in temples throughout Egypt, at Deir el-Bahari, Deir el-Medina, in the Temple of Isis at Philae, and at Thebes, where he was worshipped together with Amenhotep-son-of-Hapu, who was likewise a deified human being.

WHAT TO DO NEXT

Interest in Egyptian Paganism has been growing in recent years, but within the Pagan community as a whole, which has now become large, the number of people following the Egyptian path is still comparatively small. This can make it difficult to find suitable books on the subject, to find training courses, or to meet other devotees of Egyptian deities.

This book is intended to provide a basis for the practice of Egyptian Paganism, particularly for those who are new to it. You may feel after a while that you wish to extend your studies of Egyptian beliefs, or practice the religion in a group with others.

The Fellowship of Isis (FOI), to which we belong, runs a number of distance-learning courses and other forms of training for individuals or within groups through its network of Iseums and Lyceums. The FOI is not exclusively Egyptian-oriented, but there are groups within it dedicated to Egyptian deities and courses specializing in an Egyptian form of Pagan religion. For general information on the FOI, write (enclosing an international reply coupon) to:

> The Fellowship of Isis
> Clonegal Castle,
> Enniscorthy, Eire

For information on the FOI courses, see the Crossroads Lyceum website: http://www.fellowshipofisis.com

There are other organizations running courses in Egyptian forms of Paganism, but since we have not had experience with them, we are not in a position to comment on them. These organizations can often be found advertising in magazines on esoteric, New Age, and Pagan subjects. It is also possible to find organizations by using the Internet and typing "Egyptian gods," "Egyptian religion," the name of a deity, or any suitable word or phrase in a search engine.

It is important to always take care when approaching an organization or group for religious training. We have sometimes found that people, who would use their common sense in most situations, can become submissive and gullible when approaching someone who professes to have skills in the occult or any sort of esoteric or magical practices. This is partly because such practices are by their very nature secret, and therefore newcomers may find it hard to judge what is normal and acceptable. Use the same discretion as you would in other circumstances, and do not do anything that makes you feel uneasy, or seems to you morally wrong.

When meeting other people by joining a group, or forming your own group, it is advisable to arrange the first meeting in a café, a public house, or some other public place. It has been our experience that Pagans sometimes hold gatherings or classes in their own homes, and may invite strangers to their homes for this purpose—indeed, in the past we have done so ourselves. Unfortunately, we found out the hard way about the serious problems that can sometimes arise through taking this risk. Apart from the obvious dangers, it is a breach of the terms of a normal insurance policy, and may totally invalidate one's insurance coverage, to have members of the public, students, or clients in one's home. If you wish to carry on such an activity, you need to check with your household insurance company to make sure you have the appropriate policy or a clause added to your normal policy to protect your interests. Nowadays, to avoid having strangers in our home, we always rent a room if we wish to hold a class or Pagan meeting, and we find in any case that it is a much better environment for the purpose.

To gain a greater understanding of ancient Egyptian religion and to understand the way of thinking of these ancient people whose ideas can often seem weird from a modern point of view, it is best to go directly to the ancient material available, which will involve visiting museums with Egyptian displays, reading ancient texts (in translation), and even spending time in Egypt, if you should have the opportunity. There is really no substitute for this, as books that are a secondary source about ancient Egypt are often written from the point of view of the historian or archaeologist and provide little insight into what it would be like to experience Egyptian religion as a follower of a living faith. We suggest reading the *Pyramid Texts*, the *Coffin Texts*, and the *Book of the Dead* (listed under Budge and Faulkner in the bibliography of this book). They are difficult to understand at first, but, over time, familiarity makes them more comprehensible, especially if one already has a basic understanding of Egyptian beliefs, as we have tried to provide here.

For information on Egyptian correspondences, the best book we have found containing extensive information about this is *The Sacred Tradition in Ancient Egypt*, by Rosemary Clark, published by Llewellyn (2000). Otherwise, for magical correspondences in general, Aleister Crowley's book *777* is a classic on the subject.

If you have any queries or comments regarding Egyptian Paganism, or anything we have said in this book, please write to us.

To Write to the Author

If you wish to contact the author or would like more information about this book, please write to the author in care of Llewellyn Worldwide and we will forward your request. Both the author and publisher appreciate hearing from you and learning of your enjoyment of this book and how it has helped you. Llewellyn Worldwide cannot guarantee that every letter written to the author can be answered, but all will be forwarded. Please write to:

Jocelyn Almond & Keith Seddon
℅ Llewellyn Worldwide
P.O. Box 64383, Dept. 0-7387-0438-5
St. Paul, MN 55164-0383, U.S.A.

Please enclose a self-addressed stamped envelope for reply, or $1.00 to cover costs. If outside U.S.A., enclose international postal reply coupon.

Many of Llewellyn's authors have websites with additional information and resources.

For more information, please visit our website at
http://www.llewellyn.com

BIBLIOGRAPHY

Apuleius. *The Golden Ass / Metamorphoses.* Translated by E. J. Kenney. Includes introduction and notes. London: Penguin, 1998.

Betz, Hans Dieter, ed. *The Greek Magical Papyri in Translation.* Chicago: University of Chicago Press, 1996.

Borghouts, J. F., trans. *Ancient Egyptian Magical Texts.* Leiden: E. J. Brill, 1978.

Boylan, Patrick. *Thoth: the Hermes of Egypt.* Oxford: Oxford University Press, 1999 [1922].

Buckland, Raymond. *Buckland's Complete Book of Witchcraft.* St. Paul, MN: Llewellyn, 1987.

Budge, E. A. Wallis. *An Introduction to Ancient Egyptian Literature.* New York: Dover, 1997b. [First published in 1914 as *The Literature of the Ancient Egyptians.* London: J. M. Dent & Sons.]

————. *The Book of the Dead*. London: British Museum, Longmans & Co., 1895.

————. *The Book of the Dead*. London: Arkana, 1989.

————. *Egyptian Magic*. Reprint with new introduction. New York: Bell Publishing, 1991. [First published in 1899.]

————. *Egyptian Religion*. Secaucus, NJ: Citadel Press, 1997a. [First published in 1900.]

————. *The Gods of the Egyptians*. 2 vols. New York: Dover, 1969. [First published in 1904.]

————. *Osiris and the Egyptian Resurrection*. 2 vols. New York: Dover, 1973. [First published in 1911 by the Medici Society.]

Clark, Rosemary. *The Sacred Tradition in Ancient Egypt*. St. Paul, MN: Llewellyn, 2000.

Clark, R. T. Rundle. *Myth and Symbol in Ancient Egypt*. London: Thames and Hudson, 1978 [1959].

Cooke, Harold P. *Osiris: A Study in Myths, Mysteries and Religion*. Chicago: Ares, 1979. [First published in 1931.]

Crowley, Aleister. *777 and Other Qabalistic Writings*. Edited by Israel Regardie. York Beach, ME: Samuel Weiser, 1986.

————. *Magick*. London: Routledge & Kegan Paul, 1973.

Diodorus Siculus. *Library of History*. Vol. 1. Translated by C. H. Oldfather. [Loeb Classical Library.] Cambridge, MA: Harvard University Press., 1933.

Draco, Mélusine. *Liber Ægyptius: The Book of Egyptian Magic*. London: Ignotus Press, 1998.

Durdin-Robertson, Lawrence. *The Year of the Goddess*. Wellingborough, Northamptonshire: Aquarius, 1900.

Evans, Lorraine. *Kingdom of the Ark*. London: Simon & Schuster, 2000.

Farrar, Janet and Stewart. *Eight Sabbats for Witches*. London: Robert Hale, 1981.

————. *The Witches' Way*. London: Robert Hale, 1984. [Published in America as *A Witche's Bible*. 2 vols. New York: Magickal Childe, 1984.]

Faulkner, R. O., trans. *The Ancient Egyptian Pyramid Texts*. Warminster: Aris and Phillips, 1985. [First published in 1969. Oxford: Clarendon Press.]

———, trans. and ed. *The Ancient Egyptian Coffin Texts*. 3 vols. Warminster: Aris and Phillips, 1973.

Forrest, M. Isidora. *Isis Magic*. St. Paul, MN: Llewellyn, 2001.

Fortune, Dion. *Applied Magic and Aspects of Occultism*. London: Aquarian Press, 1987a.

———. *Esoteric Orders and their Work and the Training and Work of the Initiate*. London: Aquarian Press, 1987b.

———. *Sane Occultism and Practical Occultism in Daily Life*. London: Aquarian Press, 1987c.

Foster, John L. *Hymns, Prayers, and Songs: an Anthology of Ancient Egyptian Lyric Poetry*. Edited by Susan Tower Ellis. [Society of Bible Literature.] Atlanta, GA: Scholars Press, 1995.

Freke, Timothy and Peter Gandy. *The Jesus Mysteries*. London: Thorsons, 1999.

González-Wippler, Migene. *The Complete Book of Spells, Ceremonies and Magick*. St. Paul, MN: Llewellyn, 1988.

Griffiths, J. Gwyn, ed. *The Isis-Book (Metamorphoses, Book XI) / Apuleius of Madauros*. Leiden: E. J. Brill, 1975.

Gros de Beler, Aude. *Egyptian Mythology*. France: Molière, 1999.

Harris, Eleanor L. *Ancient Egyptian Divination and Magic*. York Beach, ME: Samuel Weiser, 1998.

Hart, George. *A Dictionary of Egyptian Gods and Goddesses*. London: Routledge and Kegan Paul, 1986.

Hermes Trismegistus. "Kore Kosmu," in *Hermetica*. [See Scott, Walter.]

Hornung, Erik. *Idea Into Image: Essays on Ancient Egyptian Thought*. Translated by Elizabeth Bredeck. Ithaca, NY: Timken, 1982.

———. *Conceptions of God in Ancient Egypt: The One and the Many*. Translated by John Baines. New York: Cornell University Press, 1996.

Ions, Veronica. *Egyptian Mythology*. London: Chancellor Press, 1997.

Bibliography

Jacq, Christian. *Egyptian Magic.* Warminster: Aris and Phillips, 1985.

———. *Fascinating Hieroglyphics.* New York: Sterling Publishing, 1997.

———. *The Living Wisdom of Ancient Egypt.* London: Simon & Schuster, 1999.

Kaplan, Aryeh. *Sefer Yetzirah: The Book of Creation.* York Beach, ME: Samuel Weiser, 1990.

Kaster, Joseph. *The Wisdom of Ancient Egypt: Writings From the Time of the Pharaohs.* London: Michael O'Mara, 1995.

Knight, Gareth. *The Practice of Ritual Magic.* Wellingborough, Great Britain: Aquarian Press, 1979.

Kraig, Donald Michael. *Modern Magick: Eleven Lessons in the High Magickal Arts.* St. Paul, MN: Llewellyn, 1988.

Lamy, Lucie. *Egyptian Mysteries: New Light On Ancient Knowledge.* London: Thames and Hudson, 1981.

Lesko, Barbara S. *The Great Goddesses of Egypt.* Norman, OK: University of Oklahoma Press, 1999.

Lichtheim, Miriam. *Ancient Egyptian Literature.* 3 vols. Berkeley: University of California Press, 1975.

Lloyd, Alan B., ed. *Studies in Pharaonic Religion and Society.* London: The Egypt Exploration Society, 1992.

Luckert, Karl W. *Egyptian Light and Hebrew Fire.* Albany, NY: State University of New York Press, 1991.

Lurker, Manfred. *Dictionary of Gods and Goddesses, Devils and Demons.* London: Routledge, 1987.

Lurker, Manfred. *An Illustrated Dictionary of The Gods and Symbols of Ancient Egypt.* London: Thames and Hudson, 1982.

Meeks, Dimitri, and Christine Farvard-Meeks. *Daily Life of the Egyptian Gods.* London: John Murray, 1997.

Naydler, Jeremy. *Temple of the Cosmos: the Egyptian Experience of the Sacred.* Rochester, VT: Inner Traditions, 1996.

Nunn, John F. *Ancient Egyptian Medicine.* London: British Museum Press, 1997.

O'Regan, Vivienne. *The Pillar of Isis.* London: Aquarian Press, 1992.

Paddon, Peter. *The Book of the Veil*. Freshfields, Chieveley: Capall Bann, 1985.

———. *Through the Veil*. Freshfields, Chieveley: Capall Bann, 1996.

Pinch, Geraldine. *Magic in Ancient Egypt*. London: British Museum Press, 1994.

Plutarch. "Isis and Osiris," in *Moralia*. Vol. 5. Translated by Frank Cole Babbitt. Cambridge, MA: Loeb Classical Library, Harvard University Press, 1936.

Reed, Ellen Cannon. *Invocation of the Gods*. St. Paul, MN: Llewellyn, 1992.

Regula, deTraci. *The Mysteries of Isis*. St. Paul, MN: Llewellyn, 1995.

Roberts, Alison. *My Heart, My Mother*. Rottingdean, England: North-Gate, 2000.

Robertson, Olivia. *The Call of Isis*. Enniscorthy, Eire: Cesara Publications, 1975.

———. *Urania: Ceremonial Magic of the Goddess*. Enniscorthy, Eire: Cesara Publications, 1983.

———. *Sophia: Cosmic Consciousness of the Goddess*. Enniscorthy, Eire: Cesara Publications, 1987.

———. *Panthea: Initiations and Festivals of the Goddess*. Enniscorthy, Eire: Cesara Publications, 1988.

Scheuler, Gerald and Betty. *Egyptian Magick: Enter the Body of Light and Travel the Magickal Universe*. St. Paul, MN: Llewellyn, 1994.

Scott, Walter, trans. Excerpt 23, "Kore Kosmu," in *Stobaei Hermetica*. Boston: Shambhala, 1993.

Shaw, Ian, and Paul Nicholson. *British Museum Dictionary of Ancient Egypt*. London: British Museum Press, 1995.

Te Velde, H. *Seth, God of Confusion*. Leiden: E. J. Brill, 1977.

Watterson, Barbara. *Gods of Ancient Egypt*. Stroud, Gloucestershire: Sutton Publishing, 1996.

——— *The House of Horus at Edfu: Ritual in an Ancient Egyptian Temple*. Stroud, Gloucestershire: Tempus, 1998.

Witt, R. E. *Isis in the Graeco-Roman World*. Ithaca, NY: Cornell University Press, 1971.

INDEX

Page numbers marked in bold type indicate chapters devoted specifically to the deities named in those entries.

Index